UNDERSTANDING SPIRITUAL GIFTS

THE OPERATION AND ADMINISTRATION OF THE GIFTS OF THE HOLY SPIRIT IN YOUR LIFE

by
Buddy Harrison

D0104572

Harrison House
Tulsa, Oklahoma

Unless otherwise indicated, all Scripture quotations are taken from the *King James Version* of the Bible.

Understanding Spiritual Gifts: The Operation and Administration of the Gifts of the Holy Spirit in Your Life
ISBN 0-57794-031-8
Copyright © 1997 by Buddy Harrison
P. O. Box 35443
Tulsa, Oklahoma 74153

Published by **Harrison House, Inc**.
P. O. Box 35035
Tulsa, Oklahoma 74153

Contents

Contents

Introduction

God desires for you as a believer to have the kind of life that is abundant, victorious and power-filled. Not all believers are walking in that fullness of life God desires for them to have.

It is becoming more and more obvious today there are two different kinds of Christians on this earth.

There are carnal ones and spiritual ones.

There are defeated ones and victorious ones.

There are Christians who follow men and Christians who follow God.

There are Christians who have life, eternal life, because having accepted Jesus as Lord, they have the Water of Life within them.

But then there are other Christians who are living the abundant life that Jesus speaks of in John 10:10 when He says, **I am come that they might have life, and that they might have it more abundantly.** The believers who are living this abundant life have the rivers of life flowing out from them to others.

It is time for the Church to wake up and realize what is available to them and what they are missing! We all have some choices to make in our lives.

I propose that you ask yourself these questions:

Which kind of Christian do I intend to be?

Where am I headed in my life?

Will I be open to receive all that Jesus has provided for me as a true believer?

Before Jesus left this earth, He told His disciples:

> **But ye shall receive power, after that the Holy Ghost is come upon you: and ye shall be witnesses unto me both in Jerusalem, and in all Judaea, and in Samaria, and unto the uttermost part of the earth.**
>
> **Acts 1:8**

Then shortly thereafter, on the Day of Pentecost the Holy Spirit descended upon the 120 believers who were waiting in the Upper Room at Jerusalem. Acts 2:4 describes what took place that day:

> **And they were all filled with the Holy Ghost, and began to speak with other tongues, as the Spirit gave them utterance.**

From that day forward, with the Holy Spirit within them, those true believers had a desire to fulfill what God had called them to do. The Spirit of God began to be manifested through them in what has become known as the "gifts of the Spirit."

If you have not already experienced the Holy Spirit manifesting His gifts through you, God is ready for you, a believer in Jesus Christ, to operate in these nine spiritual gifts as did the believers in the Early Church.

The problem is, an idea has developed in the Body of Christ — some of us think: "We've got to go to church to see those gifts manifested."

It is true that the gifts of the Spirit should be in manifestation in our churches, but we can no longer keep these gifts confined there. We need to take them beyond our church walls.

We are the Church, so wherever we are is where the Church is. We should begin to see these gifts operating through us, not just in our church building, but wherever we are. We need to recognize this so that we can start pointing ourselves in that direction.

The apostle Paul says in 2 Corinthians 10:4, **the weapons of our warfare are not carnal, but mighty through God to the pulling down of strong holds.** So we shouldn't want to operate with carnal weapons. We must be operating in spiritual gifts.

Now there are many believers who are operating in the carnal realm. They always have been and they always will be. So there will continue to be that element in the Body of Christ. All believers started out as babes in Christ, but at some point we must grow up. It is time for the Church to reach that place of maturity. We must begin to function as God would desire.

I urge you to take what is shared by me or any other minister and examine it on the basis of whether it lines up with the Word of God. Fully examine the Word of God. Don't accept something simply because somebody says it; examine it according to God's Word. Many Christians are like little birds: they will open their mouths and let anybody stuff anything down their throats. Then many of them wind up getting hurt and wonder what happened.

As Paul wrote to the Thessalonian church, **Prove all things; hold fast that which is good** (1 Thessalonians 5:21). Keep that principle in mind as we go into a discussion of the gifts of the Spirit.

I begin this study by laying a foundation for the gifts of the Spirit as found in the twelfth chapter of 1 Corinthians. There are some basic principles that we need to set down in the beginning. Then we will draw some guidelines about the gifts of the Spirit and how they work in ministry, as well as through the individual believer.

Why Spiritual Gifts?
...

Let's begin by reading a passage from 1 Corinthians, chapter 12. Beginning in the first verse, the apostle Paul says:

Now concerning spiritual gifts, brethren, I would not have you ignorant.

Ye know that ye were Gentiles, carried away unto these dumb idols, even as ye were led.

Wherefore I give you to understand, that no man speaking by the Spirit of God calleth Jesus accursed: and that no man can say that Jesus is the Lord, but by the Holy Ghost.

Now there are diversities of gifts, but the same Spirit.

And there are differences of administrations, but the same Lord.

And there are diversities of operations, but it is the same God which worketh all in all.

But the manifestation of the Spirit is given to every man to profit withal.

For to one is given by the Spirit the word of wisdom; to another the word of knowledge by the same Spirit;

To another faith by the same Spirit; to another the gifts of healing by the same Spirit;

To another the working of miracles; to another prophecy; to another discerning of spirits; to

another divers kinds of tongues; to another the
interpretation of tongues:

But all these worketh that one and the
selfsame Spirit, dividing to every man severally as
he will.

1 Corinthians 12:1-11

DON'T BE IGNORANT OF SPIRITUAL GIFTS
• • •

Notice in verse 1 of this passage Paul states that there
are spiritual gifts. He says, **Now concerning spiritual gifts,
brethren, I would not have you ignorant.**

The problem is, when it comes to these gifts of the
Spirit, most believers *are* ignorant. Now I am not saying they
are stupid, but they are ignorant.

To be ignorant means that you have a lack of knowledge
about something. In other words, you don't know about it.

Now we all will find that we are ignorant in some area of
our lives. Everybody is ignorant about something. But let me
encourage you. Don't ever get offended when somebody says
you are ignorant about something. You have to realize that
there is a difference between ignorance and stupidity. Ignorance says, "I don't know." Stupidity says, "I can't learn." It is
one thing for you not to have knowledge in your possession;
it is another thing to be so dumb that you can't learn.

The Spirit of God is not saying we are stupid; He is
saying we are ignorant of spiritual things. But Paul is telling
us here in this passage that God does not want us to be
ignorant anymore, that He does not want us to be without
knowledge. God wants us to have this knowledge in our
possession. That means it is time for us to learn — to come
into the knowledge of spiritual things.

Why is knowledge important? Because the prophet Hosea said, **My people are destroyed for lack of knowledge** (Hosea 4:6). The Church has been crippled because of a lack of knowledge of God's plan, of His will, of His ways, of what He has for us in this life. I want you to realize what 1 Corinthians, chapter 12, is saying: that God has provided the gifts of the Spirit for us, the believers.

WE NEED THESE SPIRITUAL GIFTS
...

It is important that we recognize the need for all nine gifts of the Spirit.

We cannot say that we don't have need of any of them or that we are limited to just one or two of them. The fact is, we need them all. We must avail ourselves of them whenever they would be profitable for us.

The main thing I want you to understand is that the Holy Spirit is the Author of all nine gifts, and He resides inside every believer.

So the capacity or potential is there for you as a believer to operate as God intends and thereby to be a blessing to others. You just have to trust God.

At the end of this passage in 1 Corinthians, chapter 12, Paul says, **dividing to every man severally as he** (the Spirit of God) **will** (v. 11). So, the Spirit of God divides the gifts as He wills. But not just to a few or to some. God is saying that these gifts have been given to *every* man.

THESE GIFTS ARE LIKE EQUIPMENT
• • •

It is important for you to look at these nine spiritual gifts as equipment, or tools. Now there are a lot of people who might not like for me to say that these gifts are equipment. But a spiritual gift is something that is utilized by God to work at a certain time. In other words, it is an operative thing. That is why I refer to these gifts as equipment.

You wouldn't send out a worker to dig ditches unless you gave him a shovel or the kind of equipment he would need to get the job done.

Well, God is not going to send you forth into the vineyard without giving you the equipment you would need to get your job done.

You see, it would be unjust and unfair for God to demand you to do a job without then enabling you to get that job done by giving you the capacity or the potential at least to operate.

We have to realize that these gifts are there to help us accomplish the job which God has given us to do.

God has called the believer to go into all the world and preach the Gospel to every creature, to heal the sick, to raise the dead, to cast out devils (Mark 16:15,16). In order for us to do all these things, God has to give us the necessary equipment. The Bible says God is a just God (Isaiah 45:21). He would not call us to do a job and then not give us the equipment to get that job done. Otherwise, He would be an unjust God.

Therefore, the equipment needed for the job is available to us as believers. We have read in 1 Corinthians 12:11 that God divides to every man severally as He wills. Verse 31 of

that chapter says we are to **covet earnestly the best gifts.**
What is the "best gift"? The one that is needed at the time.
When you get into a situation, you ought to be coveting the
gift that will operate at that moment and at that time.

LET GOD PUT ON A SHOW!
...

Paul wants us to realize how important the Holy Ghost
is to us. He tells us in 1 Corinthians 12:3:

> **Wherefore I give you to understand, that no
> man speaking by the Spirit of God calleth Jesus
> accursed: and that no man can say that Jesus is the
> Lord, but by the Holy Ghost.**

It takes the Holy Ghost in everything that we do. We
can't even say "Jesus is Lord" without the Holy Ghost. If we
don't become aware of the Holy Spirit and learn how He
functions, then we will miss out on being able to accomplish
anything for God.

I have news for you: this is the day that the Holy Ghost
will work. He is going to show Himself strong by demon-
strating His power through the Body of Christ. Paul said in
1 Corinthians 2:4:

> **And my speech and my preaching was not
> with enticing words of man's wisdom, but in
> demonstration of the Spirit and of power.**

God wants to put on a show through His Holy Ghost!

It is time for us in the Body of Christ to realize that He
can do it. God can demonstrate His power by showing Himself mighty and triumphant. We must realize that God is
ready to bring forth some blessings in us; and then by working through us, He can take those blessings out to others.

We in the Body of Christ should never think we have to do it all ourselves. If we were to think like that, we would get whipped every time. We are not strong enough, smart enough or good enough to accomplish this job on our own. But God has made us righteous and has equipped us through the blood of Jesus to get His job done.

It is not a matter of how "good" you are but how "right" you are. If you have been washed in the blood of Jesus, if you are walking in the Truth and the Light, then you have been made right through His work on the cross!

THE GIFTS ARE INSIDE YOU
....

Notice again Paul's words in 1 Corinthians 12:11. After listing the nine gifts of the Spirit, he says:

> **But all these worketh that one and the self-same Spirit, dividing to every man severally as he will.**

So it is by the Spirit of God that these spiritual gifts operate.

It would be wrong for a brother or sister in the Lord to brag about being able to work one or more of these spiritual gifts. A gift of the Spirit is not just something you can pull out of your back pocket whenever you want to impress other people about what you have in your possession.

Yet there is a possession sense in the fact that if God has called you to a specific office, then you require certain equipment in order to operate in that office. So at least the capacity is there, for the gifts are resident inside you and in that sense could be in your possession.

But the devil can take advantage of you if you don't know about the gifts of the Spirit, about how to operate in them and allow them to flow through you. Without such knowledge, you won't even be able to recognize them when they occur, and you certainly won't be able to get the maximum use out of them. These gifts become effective when you let them become workable tools in your life. Then you will be able to bless other people.

You must realize that these spiritual gifts are equipment that help you bless people, and the Spirit of God wants you to be knowledgeable of these gifts for that purpose.

Let's look at the gifts of the Spirit given by Paul in 1 Corinthians, chapter 12:

> **For to one is given by the Spirit the word of wisdom; to another the word of knowledge by the same Spirit;**
> **To another faith by the same Spirit; to another the gifts of healing by the same Spirit;**
> **To another the working of miracles; to another prophecy; to another discerning of spirits; to another divers kinds of tongues; to another the interpretation of tongues.**
> **1 Corinthians 12:8-10**

Now what are these nine spiritual gifts all about? Many Christians have no understanding of them.

Next we will look at some passages in John's gospel so that you can begin to see what God is wanting to bring forth into the lives of every believer today. I believe this will help you to understand the importance of these nine spiritual gifts that were given to the Body of Christ.

Jesus Brought Life
...

In John 10:10 Jesus says:

The thief (Satan) **cometh not, but for to steal, and to kill, and to destroy: I am come that they might have life, and that they might have it more abundantly.**

Satan is the thief, but Jesus came that we might have life more abundantly. Life is the beginning of all things. If you don't have life, then you are in trouble. *Big* trouble. You would be dead!

I want to take some time to lay down a very basic principle. I believe we have become so caught up in speaking about certain elements or realms, we have forgotten some basics that got us here in the first place. We have never really made a connection between two particular verses of Scripture. Let's look at them now.

In John 11, verse 25, Jesus is speaking and says:

I am the resurrection, and the life: he that believeth in me, though he were dead, yet shall he live.

There is an important point to see here. Jesus says He is the Resurrection and the Life. In John 14:6 He says, **I am the way, the truth, and the life.** So we know that Jesus is the Life.

Now look in John, chapter 1:

> In the beginning was the Word (Jesus), and the Word (Jesus) was with God, and the Word (Jesus) was God.
>
> The same was in the beginning with God.
>
> All things were made by him; and without him was not any thing made that was made.
>
> In him (Jesus) was life; and the life was the light of men.

> John 1:1-4

Verse 4 is a key verse for us. It says in Jesus there was life and that Life was the Light of men.

WHAT IS LIFE?
...

I began to meditate about life one time, asking the question, What do we mean by life?

Science defines life as correspondence with environment. For instance, when you take a fish out of water, what happens? It dies. Why? Because there is no correspondence with environment. When you take a plant out of the ground, it dies. Again, there is no correspondence with environment. If you take the spirit out of the body, what is going to happen? There would be no correspondence with environment, so death would occur.

But then what happens when somebody dead comes back to life? How do we know when someone is dead?

Medical scientists have great difficulty with this. It causes them to climb the wall when a person comes back from the dead. They don't know how to define it or what to do with it.

All that they have to go by are what they call the vital signs of life. These vital signs tell them that a person is not there. But then all of a sudden that person's heart begins to beat again. So that means there is more to it. Why? Because there is a spirit man involved with the physical body. The body may or may not have vital signs, but until the spirit has departed the body there is still life. That is what medical science seems to have forgotten.

LIFE FROM FATHER TO SON
...

In John 5, verse 26, Jesus says:

For as the Father hath life in himself; so hath he given to the Son to have life in himself.

Get a picture of what happened here between the Father and the Son.

Where does all life begin? With God the Father.

The Father had life within Himself. He gave that life to His Son so that He would have life in Himself. Then the Son came to earth and gave His life for mankind by dying on the cross and being raised from the dead. We could then be given life when we believe on Him.

Until Jesus died, there could be no resurrection. The old had to die in order to raise the new. Jesus took upon Himself sin, sickness, disease, despair and all the horrible things mankind suffered on this earth as the result of sin. He did that so you and I could be raised with Him to new life. By believing on Him, we become a new creation (2 Corinthians 5:7), a new species of being. A new element of life begins flowing in us that will make life dynamic for us.

The Bible says in 1 John 5:12 that he who has Jesus has life. So we know that in the new birth we receive Jesus and we have His life in us.

Where did we get that life? From Jesus.

Where did He get that life? From the Father.

It is important that we have that life, but more than that, we have Jesus! He is the Word, and His words produce that life.

Let's look at a passage from Proverbs, chapter 4:

> **My son, attend to my words; incline thine ear unto my sayings.**
>
> **Let them (My words) not depart from thine eyes; keep them (My words) in the midst of thine heart.**
>
> **For they (My words) are life unto those that find them, and health to all their flesh.**
>
> **Proverbs 4:20-22**

For they are life unto those that find them. This means that these words are hidden to some. So in order for people to have that life which has been hidden from them, we have to go and share it with them. Otherwise, they won't know about it.

The Father had life within Himself. He gave it to the Son so that He would have life in Himself. Then when we receive Jesus, we obtain that life in ourselves. Those words from God become real in us. Then as we grow in the spirit, we will be able to reproduce Jesus in others.

Jesus gave His life that we might have life. You see, the Father planted His Son so that He could have many sons. Why? So that they could go and give their lives to bring others to Him. As Paul wrote to the Galatian church, **the life which I now live in the flesh I live by the faith of the Son**

of God, who loved me, and gave himself for me
(Galatians 2:20). It is no longer our own life to live. We have
to live it for someone else. We have to live it in order to bless
and help others.

THE COMFORTER BRINGS FULLNESS OF LIFE
• • •

Again, in John 14:6 Jesus said, **I am the way, the truth,
and the life.** In that same chapter Jesus says in verses 14-16:

> **If ye shall ask any thing in my name, I will do
> it.**
> **If ye love me, keep my commandments.**
> **And I will pray the Father, and he shall give
> you another Comforter, that he may abide with
> you for ever.**

Now Jesus has given His life. But not only that, He has
sent us a Comforter. Look at verse 26 of John 14:

> **But the Comforter, which is the Holy Ghost,
> whom the Father will send in my name, he shall
> teach you all things, and bring all things to your
> remembrance, whatsoever I have said unto you.**

The Holy Ghost has come to teach us. He has come to
lead us into all truth. As He leads us into the fullness of life,
we will be able to have that abundant life. He will bring all
things to our remembrance so that we can then lead others
to that life.

I am covering this subject thoroughly because it is a
basic truth. If you don't make this connection, you won't see
the value of where you can be headed in the spirit realm.

The Father had life in Himself. He gave that life to His
Son Jesus so that He could have life in Himself. Then Jesus
came and gave His life here on earth so that we as sinners

could receive that life. He also wants to give us the Comforter Who will lead us into all truth.

Then out of our abundance we are to give to others. We are to take the Word of Life that the Holy Spirit moved upon men to write, and we are to share it with others. That will then bring them into the abundant life which we have found in Him.

Why does God want to bless you? So that you can be a blessing to others. If you have just your own life to live, then all you will do is live it for yourself. But if you are living the abundant life, you will have it to give to someone else. God has given you the Comforter Who will teach you; as Jesus said, He will lead you into all truth and bring all things to your remembrance.

I remember hearing the story about a woman who had been seeking the Holy Spirit. She was filled with the Holy Ghost during a Wednesday night church service. Then on Sunday morning she got up in church to testify. She was so excited. She said, "Glory to God! Glory to God! I want you all to know that I got the blanket! I got the blanket!" After a while they realized that she was talking about the Comforter. Think about it. We have been blanketed by the Holy Ghost. Isn't that what Spirit baptism really means?

SPIRIT BAPTISM
•••

There is a difference between being baptized in the Holy Spirit and being filled with the Spirit. Yet many people have not understood what the Word of God is saying about it; they have not understood the impact of it. Being baptized is one thing. Being full and fired up is something else.

22

The word *baptism* means immersion.[1] So when the Day of Pentecost came, believers got baptized in the Holy Ghost; the earth was immersed in the Holy Spirit. He is here now, so believers today can also be immersed in the Holy Ghost.

But it is one thing to be immersed into something; it is another thing to have something in you. If you were ever dunked in water, you had water all around you, didn't you? But it is different when you have received that Water of Life inside you.

As believers, we have received the Water of Life that springs up to everlasting life. But there is a place where we can get filled with the Holy Ghost. How can you tell when something is full? It runs over! What is the "running over" that occurs when a person receives the infilling of the Holy Ghost? The ability to speak in tongues.

We have the Comforter, the Holy Spirit. How did it all start? After the Father sent His Son to give His life that we could have that life, He also gave us the Comforter, the Holy Spirit. It is the Holy Spirit Who is allowing that life to be lived in us that we might have the abundant life. The Comforter will teach us and lead us into all truth. Why? So that we can then spill it out onto someone else and bring forth these blessings to other people. That is how it works.

LIFE, LIGHT, POWER
• • •

There are three basic elements that we in the Body of Christ have missed for a long time: Life, Light and Power.

---

[1] W. E. Vine, Merrill F. Unger, William White, Jr. *Vine's Complete Expository Dictionary of Old and New Testament Words.* (Nashville: Thomas Nelson, 1985), p. 50, "baptisma."

Jesus is the Life that brought Light to mankind. Remember, Scripture says in John 1:4, **In him was life; and the life was the light of men.** First, God's words produced Life, and that Life produced Light. Then the Power came when the Holy Ghost was sent on the Day of Pentecost. In Acts 1, verse 8, Jesus said, **But ye shall receive power, after that the Holy Ghost is come upon you.**

Let's look in Acts, chapter 2, at what happened to believers in the Early Church when the Holy Ghost was sent on the Day of Pentecost:

> **And when the day of Pentecost was fully come, they were all with one accord in one place.**
>
> **And suddenly there came a sound from heaven as of a rushing mighty wind, and it filled all the house where they were sitting.**
>
> **And there appeared unto them cloven tongues like as of fire, and it sat upon each (or all) of them.**
>
> **And they were all filled with the Holy Ghost, and began to speak with other tongues, as the Spirit gave them utterance.**
>
> **Acts 2:1-4**

Your first evidence of being filled with the Spirit is your faith. Hebrews 11:1 says, **Now faith is the substance of things hoped for, the evidence of things not seen.** Then the outward evidence of being filled with the Spirit is speaking in tongues.

There are always exceptions to every rule. But we are talking fundamentally. There have been some instances after a person was filled with the Spirit, the person began immediately to prophesy. But something like that happening is the exception (and a number of different things would enter in to it).

Isn't it amazing? God through Jesus has come to bring us life. But more than that, He wants to bring us into abundant life. So speaking in tongues is a way to stir and to cause that abundant life to come. Because life is in the power of the tongue, we should be excited about being able to speak in other tongues once we have been filled with the Spirit of God as had occurred on the Day of Pentecost.

The gifts of the Spirit are to be used to bring forth this Life, Light and Power to others.

Life comes by the vocal, or utterance, gifts: tongues, the interpretation of tongues and prophecy. **Death and life are in the power of the tongue** (Proverbs 18:21). Therefore, as you are speaking for God, you can know that His words will produce life.

By speaking in other tongues, I am speaking life. I can be speaking life to myself and life elements to God. When I am praying for another person, I can be speaking life elements about him and to him and bringing forth the life from God. That is moving into the abundant life, which then causes the real power to become generated.

Light is brought forth through the revelation gifts: the word of wisdom, the word of knowledge and the discerning of spirits. God, speaking through His servant, gives a word about a person's present, past or future, or provides that servant with an understanding of the spirit(s) involved with that person's life.

Power comes forth through the power gifts: faith, the working of miracles and the gifts of healings. God's Spirit works through His servant to bring a healing, to produce a miracle or to take a special step of faith.

CHAPTER 3

God Likes Variety

•••

Let's look now at another portion of Scripture from 1 Corinthians, chapter 12:

> **Now there are diversities of gifts, but the same Spirit.**
>
> **And there are differences of administrations, but the same Lord.**
>
> **And there are diversities of operations, but it is the same God which worketh all in all.**
>
> **1 Corinthians 12:4-6**

Paul is telling us here that God is a God of variety. God has many different ways of doing things in order to bring forth His blessings in the earth. He has set up different ministries in the Body of Christ.

In Ephesians, chapter 4, Paul is talking about what God has set in the Church through the work of Jesus Christ:

> **Wherefore he saith, When he ascended up on high, he led captivity captive, and gave gifts unto men.**
>
> **(Now that he ascended, what is it but that he also descended first into the lower parts of the earth?**
>
> **He that descended is the same also that ascended up far above all heavens, that he might fill all things.)**
>
> **Ephesians 4:8-10**

Notice it says in verse 8 that Jesus ascended up on high and gave gifts to men. So, when certain people are called of God, they are given gifts, which we call ministry gifts. Paul goes on in this passage to say:

> **And he gave some, apostles; and some, prophets; and some, evangelists; and some, pastors and teachers;**
>
> **For the perfecting of the saints, for the work of the ministry, for the edifying of the body of Christ:**
>
> **Till we all come in the unity of the faith, and of the knowledge of the Son of God, unto a perfect man, unto the measure of the stature of the fulness of Christ.**
>
> **Ephesians 4:11-13**

These ministry gifts are broken into five basic categories. They are listed in verse 11 as apostles, prophets, evangelists, pastors and teachers. Yet there are more than that. Notice what is stated in 1 Corinthians 12:27,28:

> **Now ye are the body of Christ, and members in particular.**
>
> **And God hath set some in the church, first apostles, secondarily prophets, thirdly teachers, after that miracles, then gifts of healings, helps, governments, diversities of tongues.**

Paul continues in this passage by asking a series of questions about these gifts. He says:

> **Are all apostles? are all prophets? are all teachers? are all workers of miracles?**
>
> **Have all the gifts of healing? do all speak with tongues? do all interpret?**
>
> **But covet earnestly the best gifts: and yet shew I unto you a more excellent way.**
>
> **1 Corinthians 12:29-31**

Before going any further, let's answer each of Paul's questions in this passage:

Are all apostles?

No.

Are all prophets?

No.

Are all teachers?

No.

Are all workers of miracles?

No.

Have all the gifts of healing?

No.

Do all speak with tongues?

No.

Do all interpret?

No.

Now notice especially one of Paul's questions. In verse 30 he asks: **Do all speak with tongues?** Immediately, people of various denominations will take this one question by itself and argue defensively, "See, it says right here that everybody doesn't speak with tongues!" But this has to be read in the context of what is being discussed in this passage.

You see, Paul isn't talking about the simple gift of tongues, which every believer receives when he is baptized with the Holy Spirit. Every Spirit-filled believer can speak with tongues. As Scripture says, **For he that speaketh in an unknown tongue speaketh not unto men, but unto**

God...He that speaketh in an unknown tongue edifieth himself (1 Corinthians 14:2,4).

Paul is talking in 1 Corinthians 12:30 about the ministry gift of tongues, and not everybody has that ministry gift.

Now understand that ministry gifts are gifts from God to the Church.

For what purpose?

To build up the Body of Christ, to edify the saints, to preach the Good News, or glad tidings, to the world.

As God's children, we have a job to do. We have been given a commission. Jesus spoke the Great Commission to the Church in Mark, chapter 16:

> **Go ye into all the world, and preach the gospel to every creature.**
> **He that believeth and is baptized shall be saved; but he that believeth not shall be damned.**
> **And these signs shall follow them that believe; In my name shall they cast out devils; they shall speak with new tongues;**
> **They shall take up serpents; and if they drink any deadly thing, it shall not hurt them; they shall lay hands on the sick, and they shall recover.**
> **Mark 16:15-18**

Then God gave His children the equipment to carry out the job, to accomplish it, to get it done.

What is that equipment?

The nine gifts of the Spirit.

In most instances, God intends for the gifts of the Spirit to be a way for the Church to operate out there in the world and be able to help unbelievers. Yet, most of the time these gifts occur strictly within our church walls.

Now, of course, every minister or pastor should be furnished the necessary equipment in order for him to be able to work more freely and more proficiently within his own ministry or church. Yet, the gifts of the Spirit have the capacity to operate in any Spirit-filled believer, and these gifts should be working for each of us out in the world.

So you, the believer, should expect God to equip you. If He has called you to bring sinners in and to have life ministered to them, then those gifts of the Spirit potentially should operate in your ministry whenever you have need of them.

Again, 1 Corinthians 12:11 says, **But all these worketh that one and the selfsame Spirit, dividing to every man severally as he will.** Therefore, you can have a confidence. You can know that, when you meet the world out there and come face-to-face with a situation, God will cause the gift that is needed to rise up inside you. But you have to recognize it and have faith for it. You have to expect the Holy Spirit to present you with the gift you need at that time in order for you to be able to utilize and operate as He wills.

So you can see the gifts working in two areas, two categories: through the ministry gifts to believers in the Church and through the gifts of the Spirit operating in believers to reach the world, lead sinners to hear the message and to accept the saving grace of the Lord Jesus Christ.

That doesn't mean it can't work where just one believer ministers to another believer. It can. But the ultimate of why God has given that gift to you is for you to utilize it out in the world to help you win the lost and bring them to Jesus.

There is certain equipment designed to help make each of these ministry gifts work more proficiently. For example, whoever heard of a prophet who didn't prophesy? So, that prophetic gift would be in his possession. God will equip him and make him ready to get the job done as His prophet.

Let's look now into the subject of operating and administering the gifts of the Spirit.

Operation and Administration of Spiritual Gifts
...

Again, 1 Corinthians 12:4-6 says:

Now there are diversities of gifts, but the same Spirit.

And there are differences of administrations, but the same Lord.

And there are diversities of operations, but it is the same God which worketh all in all.

DIFFERENCES OF ADMINISTRATIONS
...

As we have seen listed in Ephesians 4:11, there are the fivefold ministry gifts, as well as those mentioned in 1 Corinthians 12:28, and there are various ways in which these gifts are administrated.

In 1 Corinthians 12:5 where it gives the word *administrations*, in the margin of most Bibles there is the word *ministries*. In other words, different ministries operate different ways. God takes that person's personality, ability and knowledge and uses it according to his or her level.

We can see this occurring in politics. For instance, when Republicans go into office, they govern one way while Democrats govern another. If the Independents had control, they would run it another way. In any case, it is still the same government with the same rules and regulations. But with a different administration, there will be a difference as to how the government is operated.

The same is true with the gifts of the Spirit.

There can be different ministries and different churches with the same Spirit of God behind them, but they each could have a different way of administration. This ministry over here puts an emphasis on one thing while that ministry over there puts an emphasis on something else. Different churches will operate in the gifts in different ways. That doesn't mean that any are wrong, as long as they are using the principle of God's Word as the guideline.

The problem is, when difference comes, we have a tendency to be negative. We look at a ministry or a church and think that if it doesn't fit our rules, then it must be wrong.

We are so used to working by certain formulas, we say, "Now, brother, if it doesn't work here, and here, and here, and here, then it can't be God." But I have news for you: it *can* be!

As I had pointed out in my last chapter, God uses variety in life. If you don't think He does, just look around at the different faces in the Body of Christ. It is all the same Spirit of God, but He will be manifested one way through one individual and another way through another individual.

DIVERSITIES OF OPERATIONS
• • •

Have you ever noticed how various ministries differ from one another? One ministry will emphasize faith, while another emphasizes love, and still another emphasizes the supernatural. There may be a variety of emphases, but it is still the same Spirit, isn't it? It is still the same God, isn't it?

So when you see something in a different vein, it is important that you not be critical or negative toward it. Instead, begin to examine it in light of God's Word. Ask yourself: Does it line up with God's Word? Does it meet the criteria of the Word? It may not be your flavor, but it still can be okay.

Stop and think about it. When you go into an ice cream shop, there will be many different flavors of ice cream that you can choose from. You may not be particularly crazy about pistachio, but other people will go wild about it. Isn't that right?

You will find then there are differences of operations because different people like different aspects of ministry.

How the Holy Spirit operates through various individuals will differ from person to person, depending upon their personality, their abilities, their vocabulary and their own experiences. That simply means that different individuals will operate the same gift in different styles. In other words, they will know how to yield to it differently.

Therefore, you will see a variance as to how the gifts operate and how they move in different people. If one person is very quiet and demure, the Spirit of God will operate through that person in a certain way. Let me give you an example.

AN EXAMPLE OF DIVERSITY
...

I remember the first time I saw Sister Jeanne Wilkerson minister. She was a petite woman who was really anointed of God. I had never seen anybody quite like her. Sometimes she could sound like a foghorn. There was one time when I telephoned her for prayer support.

I was working with Kenneth Hagin's ministry then. I had been preaching weekend meetings and holding a Bible study for quite a while, but I was getting ready to go out and conduct my first full-fledged meeting.

The enemy had been beating me over the head and whipping at me about a particular area of my life. Whenever I turned around, I could hear the devil's degrading voice, saying over and over, "You're nothing but a parrot repeating what you heard. You're nothing but a parrot repeating what you heard." The way he said that sounded to me just like a parrot. It was irritating and frustrating.

Somehow in my heart, I felt that I should call Sister Wilkerson. That was the only time I ever did it. When she answered the phone, I said, "Sister Wilkerson, this is Buddy Harrison. I'm going out to hold my first meeting, and I had the desire for you to pray with me over the phone concerning this meeting. Would you do that?"

"I would be glad to," she said. Then she began to pray.

In a little while I heard the volume rising in her voice. Then I knew that the Spirit of God was about to move in on the scene. She had been praying in tongues, then these words came out of her mouth: "You're not a parrot! You're not a parrot! You know what you know, so preach what you know!"

That was a different operation of the Spirit of God. The word that was given to me from the Spirit just liberated me! Glory to God!

Now there are other people who can quietly and politely deliver a word that the Spirit of God has given to them. So this just shows the differences of operations. It is the same Spirit, the same Lord, Who is working in each and every individual as they avail themselves of the Spirit of God. Thanks be to God that He has a variety. He knows the kind of operation that will reach our hearts and penetrate us and bless our lives.

It seems this variety in God has been blocked by people who have gotten comfortable and who don't like change. They want to box in everything. They may try to pigeonhole the Holy Ghost, but that is hard to do. He can go in so many different directions. He has a variety of ways He can operate in and through our lives.

Your Spirit Will Bear Witness
• • •

As Scripture says in 1 Corinthians 12:4-6, there are diversities of gifts, differences of administrations and diversities of operations. Each of the gifts has a different function. They will be geared to a certain area in order to accomplish a specific thing.

You might ask, "How will I know whether or not it's God?"

Your spirit bears witness that you are a child of God, right? Then the same principle can apply here. The Spirit of God within you can bear witness whether it is God's Spirit that is in operation. If not, it will be the way it was described by Paul in 1 Corinthians 13:1, **as sounding brass, or a tinkling cymbal.** You can just know that it is not right.

You might say, "Well, what if I don't know? What if I haven't trained to the point where I will know whether or not it's God?"

The Bible says, **Prove all things; hold fast that which is good** (1 Thessalonians 5:21). You have to take the Word of God and find out if what you see and hear lines up with the Word. Paul said, **There are, it may be, so many kinds of voices in the world, and none of them is without significance** (1 Corinthians 14:10). They all may have meaning, and they all may have direction.

You have to begin to zero in on it and determine where that voice is coming from: Is it coming from the outside, or is it coming from the inside? With the Spirit of God inside you, it will come from there. But if it is coming from the outside, it could be from the devil, from the world or from your own head.

So, you have to filter it. It would help for you to set up a way where you can begin to check it out, to prove it, to establish it.

GOD DESIRES FOR THE GIFTS
TO OPERATE THROUGH YOU!
• • •

Look at 1 Corinthians, chapter 12, verse 7:

> **But the manifestation of the Spirit is given to every man to profit withal.**

This means simply that every believer in Jesus has the capacity to operate in the gifts of the Spirit. The potential for it is there if you are filled with the Spirit.

The Holy Ghost is given to every man, just as it says in 1 Corinthians, chapter 12, verse 11: that the Spirit of God divides to every man severally as He wills. We don't have to lose. Thank God for that!

For years you may have been saying, "I know the gifts of the Spirit are going to operate, but only through the fivefold ministry gifts." Realize that as a believer you can start making them personal.

OPEN YOURSELF TO GOD
...

Determine right now that the gifts are going to operate through you. Say, "I'm ready, God. I want to be a vessel You can work through."

Open yourself to receive the gift (or gifts) that God desires to operate through you. When the need arises, you can know it right then. There can be a witness in your heart. There can be a knowing inside you that it is the voice of God because you are a child of God.

In Acts, chapter 9, God told Ananias to go and lay hands on Saul (later known as Paul). When God said that, Ananias may well have responded with words like this: "Lord, I appreciate this opportunity, but I've heard about that guy. He's out there putting Christians in jail. So I think I'll pass." (This of course is my loose translation of what took place, but it is still true.) Ananias didn't want to get involved with Saul because of all the trouble he had caused Christians. But God told Ananias that Saul was a chosen vessel; in other words, that Saul would be an instrument for God.

Let me give you an example. A pulpit is an instrument. But it is an inanimate object that has no feelings, so it doesn't care how it is used. When we reach the point that we don't have any feelings about how we will be used by God, then we can be usable. The problem is, most of us have feelings. We might even tell God how we want to be used!

You must have the desire to be an instrument of God. Be like a musical instrument. Let God play you; He can make beautiful music through you. God will bring it forth.

So as the Scripture says, the manifestation of God's Spirit is given to every man to profit withal. God wants us to profit through His gifts; He doesn't want us to lose out.

AN EXAMPLE OF TONGUES AND INTERPRETATION THAT OCCURRED IN PUBLIC
• • •

Where you end up ministering in the gifts of the Spirit might be surprising. I remember one time when the gifts of tongues and interpretation operated through Pat and me right out in public.

We had been holding meetings in California at Ed Dufresne's church. Ed and I have done a number of meetings together with Happy Caldwell and Jerry Savelle. After our meetings there, the four of us with our families had gone to Knott's Berry Farm, where there were lots of rides and some great restaurants. We were having a fun time of fellowship, just glad we could be together.

As we were having a meal in one of the restaurants, Happy and Jeannie were talking about how God was dealing with them to go back to Little Rock, Arkansas, to start a work there. One of the things Jeannie had been concerned about was that they had pastored in Little Rock years before and people might see it as destruction for them to come back home.

40

All of a sudden, sitting right there at the table, with people walking by on each side of us, Pat pointed her finger at Happy and Jeannie and started talking in tongues. When she finished that message in tongues, I began to give the interpretation. We didn't care if people were walking by. That didn't make any difference to us.

The Spirit of the Lord said, "Yes, you'll go back to Little Rock, and you'll build a church, and you'll affect the whole city. That which you thought was meant for destruction is going to be meant for construction."

Today their church is located in the most beautiful part of town. They have built a million-dollar church building, which they paid cash for, and they are running about 1,500 people in their Sunday morning services.

God is really using them in an amazing way. Not only is Happy preaching on TV, but they also run a children's program on TV. They got the Playboy channel thrown off in their city!

How did all of that come about?

By our willingness to obey God's Spirit and to allow the Holy Ghost to move through us as we were sitting there in that restaurant.

What did God do for them?

He brought Life, Light and Power to meet their need.

Now let's look in more detail at the nine spiritual gifts that have been given to the Body of Christ.

Nine Gifts of the Spirit

Let's look again in 1 Corinthians, chapter 12. Here Paul lists the nine gifts of the Spirit:

> For to one is given by the Spirit the word of wisdom; to another the word of knowledge by the same Spirit;
>
> To another faith by the same Spirit; to another the gifts of healing by the same Spirit;
>
> To another the working of miracles; to another prophecy; to another discerning of spirits; to another divers kinds of tongues; to another the interpretation of tongues.
>
> **1 Corinthians 12:8-10**

There are nine different gifts of the same Spirit. These nine gifts are broken down into three fundamental categories: the vocal gifts, the revelation gifts and the power gifts.

There are three groups of three. With three being considered the perfect number, these nine gifts of the Spirit would be perfection times perfection.

THE VOCAL GIFTS
· · ·

The three vocal, or utterance, gifts are:

Divers kinds of tongues

The interpretation of tongues

The gift of prophecy

These vocal gifts speak words that will edify, exhort and comfort the hearer.

THE REVELATION GIFTS
· · ·

The three revelation gifts are:

The word of wisdom

The word of knowledge

The discerning of spirits

These revelation gifts reveal or make known something and cause a person to see or to know the truth about another individual or a situation.

THE POWER GIFTS
· · ·

The three power gifts are:

Faith

Miracles

The gifts of healings

These power gifts are action gifts which will cause someone to do or accomplish something.

THE VALUE CATEGORY
· · ·

You have to understand that there is a value category involved with these spiritual gifts. (I will explain in more detail later.) Some of them have more value or more importance than others.

The revelation gifts are of the highest value.

The power gifts are of the second value.

The vocal gifts are of the third value.

As we have read in 1 Corinthians 12:1, Paul wrote that he did not want us to be ignorant concerning the fact that there are spiritual gifts. You must realize that these spiritual gifts are not natural gifts. Now the natural part of man can enter in through the vocal gifts because the human is involved in these gifts by cooperating with the Spirit of God.

There is very little instruction in the Word of God on the power gifts or the revelation gifts. There are, however, instructions concerning the vocal gifts because they require a mutual cooperation between the speaker and the Holy Spirit. In other words, it takes you using your lips and your tongue and lifting your voice to speak a message in tongues, to give the interpretation or to prophesy. Therefore, there are some instructions needed in this area because these gifts can be misused and abused.

Now there are elements involved in using these gifts, and faith is a part of it. You should be looking to God, expecting Him to be gracious enough to use you, and you must have a confidence to know that He *will* use you. Yet the gifts are still going to operate as the Spirit wills.

STEPS TO TAKE WHEN OPERATING IN THESE GIFTS
• • •

God does things on a graduated basis. There are steps for us to take as we grow into things. But many Christians don't realize or understand this. For instance, we grow in faith. As we continue to operate in faith, then we will graduate on into the other spiritual principles that God wants us to know about.

The first step we are to take in these spiritual gifts is to operate in the vocal gifts. The next step would be for us to operate in the revelation gifts, and then in the power gifts.

The vocal gifts are the least. But please don't misunderstand me. I am not belittling them.

It would be like the difference between the $1 bill and the $100 bill. There are more $1 bills used daily in our society than there are $100 bills. The $1 bills are valuable, but the $100 bills are even more valuable.

The vocal gifts are like a $1 bill, while the revelation gifts are more like a $100 bill. Of the three groups then, the revelation gifts have the highest value.

I want you to see that we are dealing with an element in which we grow in God's ways. We begin with the three vocal gifts, and that then leads us on into the revelation gifts. Now the revelation gifts are more important than the power gifts, because it usually takes the revelation gifts to get us into the power gifts. We need revelation on how and where we are to extend the power of God, where it is to be placed.

DON'T GAUGE A PERSON'S SPIRITUALITY
BY HOW HE OPERATES IN THE GIFTS
• • •

One thing I want you to understand: don't use someone's operation in the gifts of the Spirit as a spiritual yardstick to gauge how spiritual that person is. That has nothing to do with it.

There are too many instances, even in the Word of God, where people who were carnal were still used in the things of God.

For example, the church at Corinth was probably one of the most carnal churches at the time. They were mightily used in the gifts of the Spirit; they operated proficiently in them, particularly the vocal gifts. Yet, many of the men in that day cohabited with their step-mother. The truth is, they were living in adultery and were still being used in the gifts of the Spirit.

You might ask, "Can that really be?"

Yes. An example of it can be found in 1 Corinthians 5:1,2. And I am sad to say, there are still examples of such things today.

But that doesn't make it right. It certainly doesn't make it good.

The better and cleaner the human vessel is, the more pure the gift will be. That is why we as God's people should be living a clean life. We should be separating and sanctifying ourselves **with the washing of water by the word** (Ephesians 5:26). Then our lives will become pure and we won't be picking up any of the other elements of life.

LIVING IN SIN WON'T NECESSARILY STOP SOMEONE FROM BEING ABLE TO OPERATE IN THE GIFTS
• • •

Yet you say, "Do you really believe that somebody could be living in sin and still operate in the gifts?"

Yes, I know they can. I have seen it, not only in my lifetime but in God's Word.

Look at Jonah. He was in a backslidden condition, yet God still used him.

Then there was Saul. There were times when he would get out among the soothsayers and yield to their ways; yet when he came back among the people of God, he would yield to the Spirit of God. You see, Saul knew how to yield.

Many times people will say, "How can those who are carnal or backslidden move in the gifts of the Spirit?"

They can do it because they know how to yield and to cooperate with the Spirit of God. Remember what it says in God's Word: **For the gifts and calling of God are without repentance** (Romans 11:29). You see, God does not change His mind.

Many times there have been ministers who have had the call of God on their lives; they have known how to yield to the Spirit of God in a given situation, yet at the same time have not lived their own personal lives as God would have desired.

Now that may shock you. I am not trying to paint a bad picture. I just want you to understand that you can't use the gifts of the Spirit as a yardstick to measure spirituality. It just doesn't work that way. Being able to operate in a spiritual gift is not a sign of that person's spirituality. All it means is that he or she knows how to yield to the Spirit of God.

We all should take a lesson and be learning from this. We should be living our lives clean. But we can also learn how to yield and therefore be mightily used of God.

Now I will make a statement here that may shock you: the gifts of the Spirit can operate through those who are not filled with the Spirit. There are only two of the nine spiritual gifts that they could not operate in: tongues and interpretation of tongues. These two gifts are New Testament dispensation gifts, but all the other gifts operated under the Old Testament, the Old Covenant, and the people in those days weren't even born again.

You can check this out for yourself by looking into God's Word, both the Old Testament and the New. Examine the lives of those people who were using the gifts of the Spirit, and you will be able to see this more readily.

Let's break it down now and look at each of these three groups of spiritual gifts, beginning with the vocal gifts.

The Vocal Gifts:
Tongues and Interpretation of Tongues
• • •

For to one is given by the Spirit...prophecy; to another...divers kinds of tongues; to another the interpretation of tongues.

1 Corinthians 12:8,10

The vocal gifts, which will be discussed first, are divers kinds of tongues, interpretation of tongues and prophecy. These vocal gifts are the ecstatic gifts of utterance, or gifts of inspiration.

God specifically says that these gifts of inspiration were given to the Church of Jesus Christ by the Holy Spirit. They are designed to edify, build up and strengthen the Church. With these vocal gifts, we witness the remarkable power of words that are anointed and inspired by the Holy Ghost.

Certainly in this present hour, there are multitudes of Christians who are in great need of having their spiritual lives built up and strengthened. This is no doubt the reason why the apostle Paul spoke in tongues more than the entire Corinthian church (1 Corinthians 14:18). He desired to be "built up," and his practice of speaking in tongues was one of the secrets of his amazing strength.

Some Bible teachers have intimated that these vocal, or inspirational, gifts are so small that they are almost unnecessary. Even to think such a thing would be a reproach against God because He chose to set these spiritual gifts in the Church. It is our duty to accept all of them.

DIVERS KINDS OF TONGUES
. . .

The gift of divers kinds of tongues is a supernatural utterance from God. It is divine and spiritual communication, a verbal or vocal miracle. With this gift, man speaks directly to God through his spirit by using a spirit language.

What a joy it is when we can speak to God personally and directly. But this is perhaps the most misunderstood of all the spiritual gifts.

THE FIRST STEP CAME AT PENTECOST

The ability to speak in tongues came into being on the Day of Pentecost as is described in Acts 2:4:

> **And they were all filled with the Holy Ghost, and began to speak with other tongues, as the Spirit gave them utterance.**

This unique ability to speak in tongues has been identified only with the Church of Jesus Christ since its inception. From that day, God has provided believers with the power of the Holy Ghost and has given us the ability and authority to speak in tongues. This ability enables us, then, to become even more powerful and more dynamic for reaching out to others.

This simple gift of speaking in tongues was *prophesied by Jesus* in Mark 16:17:

> And these signs shall follow them that believe...they shall speak with new tongues.

There is no doubt or ambiguity with Jesus.

In 1 Corinthians 14:5 Paul said he wished that everyone would speak in tongues.

When you are praying in tongues, or praying in the Spirit, you are praying the perfect prayer, a prayer that will always be according to the will of the Father. One Scripture says that praying in the Spirit is a way for you to give thanks well (1 Corinthians 14:17). Why? Because there is no selfishness in it.

One must first experience Acts 2:4 and speak in tongues personally before the Church gift of divers kinds of tongues can operate. Only Spirit-filled Christians are candidates for this gift.

TONGUES ARE A WAY TO SPEAK TO GOD

The ability to speak in tongues is not the result of learning foreign languages. The person who speaks a message in tongues has no knowledge or understanding of what he is saying. His spirit is speaking to God. Paul states this in 1 Corinthians, chapter 14, verse 2:

> For he that speaketh in an unknown tongue speaketh not unto men, but unto God.

This gift flows from the spirit of man, not from his mind. Again, Paul says:

> For if I pray in an unknown tongue, my spirit prayeth, but my understanding is unfruitful.
>
> 1 Corinthians 14:14

This gift is a special challenge and sign to those who are uninformed. So it has no relationship with the human mind.

TONGUES ARE A SIGN TO THE SINNER

The gift of tongues is a sign to the sinner. In 1 Corinthians 14:22 Paul says:

> **Wherefore tongues are for a sign, not to them that believe, but to them that believe not.**

WHEN TONGUES ARE FORBIDDEN IN CHURCH

The offering of a message in tongues is forbidden in a church service when that message comes without interpretation. This point is made in 1 Corinthians 14:28 when Paul says:

> **If there be no interpreter, let him keep silence in the church; and let him speak to himself, and to God.**

Notice, however, that the practice of speaking in tongues privately is not prohibited, only the speaking forth of a message to an entire congregation when no interpretation can be given.

"FORBID NOT THIS GIFT"

Church leaders are told not to forbid this gift.

> **Wherefore, brethren, covet to prophesy, and forbid not to speak with tongues.**
>> **1 Corinthians 14:39**

Paul says in verse 5 of this chapter:

> **I would that ye all spake with tongues....**

WHEN WILL TONGUES CEASE?

> **...whether there be tongues, they shall cease....**
>> **1 Corinthians 13:8**

The Holy Spirit is particularly identified with the Church. Has the Church age ended? There is no Bible intimation of a change from the day the Church was born until the Rapture occurs — when Jesus calls for believers to be taken from earth to heaven.

Tongues will cease at the end of this age when knowledge shall vanish and the Church will have been taken to heaven with our Lord.

WHY WILL TONGUES CEASE?

When we are in heaven, we will no longer need for the Holy Spirit to guide us into truth. We will speak the same language as Jesus. (John 14:26.)

There will be no need for tongues as a sign to unbelievers; there will be no unbelievers in heaven. (1 Corinthians 14:22.)

We will no longer have need for unknown tongues to glorify God or to edify ourselves when we are in heaven.

THE GIFT OF TONGUES TAKES LITTLE FAITH

Of the vocal gifts, the one that takes the least amount of faith is divers kinds of tongues. It actually takes more faith to interpret than it does just to speak a message in tongues.

You will find that, for the most part, the gift of tongues is the first gift of the Spirit in which people will usually operate. This is a way God has of making a direct link and hookup to graduate us right on into the other spiritual gifts.

The person speaking in tongues should seek the second gift of interpretation. Paul says:

> **Wherefore let him that speaketh in an unknown tongue pray that he may interpret.**
>
> **1 Corinthians 14:13**

You should see that God desires for you to move on into the realm of the supernatural. Speaking in tongues is the first step in that direction because speaking in tongues is supernatural.

What most people don't know is that there is a difference between the supernatural and the spectacular. Some of the other spiritual gifts are more spectacular, and we will see this in more depth as we study the other gifts.

A lot of times we think that if the spectacular doesn't happen, then the supernatural hasn't occurred. If we are not careful, we will miss the power essence of what God is trying to bring forth in our lives. You see, God can begin to move in certain places and circles by operating in ways that we had not thought about.

So the least of the nine gifts of the Spirit is divers kinds of tongues.

THE INTERPRETATION OF TONGUES
• • •

The gift of the interpretation of tongues is a supernatural presentation by God's Spirit of the meaning of an utterance that was spoken by a person in a language he does not understand.

ITS PURPOSE

The purpose of this gift is to render a message from Christ. The message is given first in an unintelligible tongue. Then a person who is led to obey the Spirit of God speaks in a language that is intelligible to those present. This interpretation is given to edify the Church.

The gift of interpretation also exalts the Lord Jesus Christ. It is the functioning of a miracle which can be seen easily by the unbeliever, causing consternation within him, as we saw happening on the Day of Pentecost when the Church was born.

Interpretation of tongues has a higher value than speaking in tongues. Notice Paul's words in 1 Corinthians, chapter 14:

> **For he that speaketh in an unknown tongue speaketh not unto men, but unto God: for no man understandeth him; howbeit in the spirit he speaketh mysteries.**
>
> **1 Corinthians 14:2**

It is vital then that a message given in tongues before a group of believers be interpreted **that the church may receive edifying** (1 Corinthians 14:5). Further along in chapter 14, Paul says, **let him that speaketh in an unknown tongue pray that he may interpret** (v. 13).

WHAT AN INTERPRETATION IS NOT

Another point you must realize concerning interpretation of tongues is that it is not a translation of the language spoken in tongues, but rather gives forth the meaning that is intended. The message in tongues could be long, while the interpretation of tongues is short, or vice versa.

The interpretation of tongues is not an operation of the human mind but is a functioning of the Holy Spirit through the mind. The interpreter does not understand the language he is interpreting, so his mental faculties can have no control over the message.

When giving an interpretation of tongues, the interpreter normally receives only one or two words in the beginning. Then as he speaks those first words, the remainder of the message will come to him, perhaps only a few words at a time. The interpreter has no thought in his own mind as to what the Spirit has to say. The message he presents is coming from his spirit, not his mind.

AN EXAMPLE OF TONGUES AND INTERPRETATION
· · ·

A tremendous illustration of the fruit of this gift took place one time when I had preached in Washington, DC. After my sermon, a message was given in tongues by one brother and another brother had interpreted it. A young man, who was in the back of the building, heard that message and was intrigued by it.

When they were finished, this young man walked to the front, approached the man who had given the message in tongues and began speaking to him in a foreign language. But the brother interrupted him, saying, "I'm sorry, sir. I don't understand any other language than English. I am a car salesman here in Washington."

The young man then responded to him in English: "But you spoke my language beautifully. I am a Persian, and I am here selling Persian carpets. You were speaking my language and you told me that I must get right with God, that I must find God now."

The brother answered, "No, that was the Spirit of God speaking to you, not me."

To the young man's surprise, neither of the two men who had been involved in that message spoke or understood his language.

As a result of the operation of the gifts of tongues and interpretation that night, the young man knelt at the altar and gave his heart to the Lord Jesus Christ.

What a joyous presentation of God's love to the world through the gifts of the Spirit!

THE VALUE OF SPIRITUAL TRAINING
* * *

One of the people I dearly loved to hear giving an interpretation in tongues was Brother Charles Duncombe. He had a vocabulary that just sent me into seventh heaven. He could use some of the most fantastic words. I might need a dictionary, but I loved the clarity that rang in his ministry. He had operated for years with a proficiency that just flowed out of him, like water running out of a spigot.

Brother Duncombe would begin to minister by talking about the spirit of fear. He might say: "For God has not given you the spirit of fear but of power and of love and of a sound mind. There is no reason why you should be fearful and remain in that condition any longer, for God hath liberated you and made you free." He would speak these words in a deep, strong voice, and it would be dynamic as that anointing was flowing through him.

Now it can be the same Spirit of God moving on somebody else who doesn't have that personality or that vocabulary; he just stands and says, "God doesn't want you scared!" It would be wrong for me to say that this person was not speaking from the same Spirit because his vocabulary was different and he ministered in a simpler fashion. You see, the same Spirit of God would be using him, according to his personality, his vocabulary and his ability.

They both made the same point, didn't they? And their message came across, didn't it?

A person who hasn't ministered very much might be shaking and trembling, but when he recognizes that God is leading him, he will want to obey.

Don't be critical when you see one of these gifts in operation, particularly in a novice.

Consider a person who is first learning how to drive. He might read the manual to find out what he should do. But it will be entirely different when he gets behind the steering wheel and takes off down the road. It would not be wise for him to try to learn how to drive in busy downtown traffic at five o'clock on a weekday afternoon. He might learn, but somebody could get hurt in the process.

The same would be true of a spiritual amateur who has never operated in the gifts of the Spirit.

Suppose he were in a service where thousands of people were being led by those who are proficiently used by the Spirit of God. It would be dangerous for that layman to try to operate a spiritual gift in that kind of meeting. By not knowing how to cooperate and to flow with it, he could end up getting hurt. It is not that he doesn't have good intentions, but he must learn how to guide his desire to operate in the gifts and know how to work with it.

So much of the time, such people have not been given ample opportunity to learn how to operate in the gifts of the Spirit. They have been kept in a box to the point that they are limited and held back. Then if they wait until they are in a crowd of people, the desire to operate that gift will be ringing so loudly in their ears that they feel it will just explode inside them if they don't get it out.

The smart thing would be for them to get into a small Bible study or small prayer group where they can begin to learn how to operate in these gifts. Then there will be people around them who can understand and can help them. Even if they do happen to head off in the wrong direction, there won't be nearly as many people who might get hurt as a result.

It is the same Spirit of God at work in them, but as we have read from 1 Corinthians 12:6, there are differences of operations.

The person who is first learning how to drive can either get out on those back roads or head into downtown traffic at the five-o'clock rush. Some people will develop and be skillful enough to actually become like race-car drivers. They will be able to drive at high speeds consistently and win. But there will be many others who would be better off just driving back and forth to work.

DECENTLY AND IN ORDER
. . .

Now there are keys or guidelines to operating in the gifts of the Spirit. That is why you have to use principles in the Word of God — not formulas.

The principle involved with tongues and interpretation is that every man profits withal. We found that principle in 1 Corinthians 12:7. But the Bible also says, **Let all things be done decently and in order** (1 Corinthians 14:40).

Suppose you were in a big meeting where there were 1,000 or 2,000, maybe even 10,000 people. Let's say a lady stands in the back of the auditorium and in her sweet, soft voice begins to give an utterance in tongues. Then another person gives the interpretation with a similarly sounding voice. Maybe a third of the congregation were able to hear that message.

Another individual who heard it knows the voice of God, and he witnesses that it was the Spirit of God. But even if it were the Spirit of God, it still was not right because of order. That is when it became unscriptural.

You might say, "But I thought you said it was the Spirit of God?"

That's right; it was. Maybe those involved know the voice of God, have heard from God and have used a legitimate gift, but it became unscriptural when all of those present did not profit from it. Do you follow me?

The way the gifts operate in a group of twenty will be different from how they will operate in a group of 2,000. It then requires a different operation. You cannot make an operation fit in another category.

When you are in a big crowd, it becomes important that tongues and interpretation be where all can hear; then all will profit. If all do not hear, it is not in order.

When I was pastoring Faith Christian Fellowship and 1,000 people were attending Sunday mornings, we developed a particular way of operation in order to handle that many people. We simply told everybody, "If you have something from God, raise your hand and you will be recognized. If you are not recognized, just trust those who are in leadership at that time."

We did not allow somebody to stand and give an utterance back in the corner of the sanctuary. We asked that person to raise his or her hand, wait to be recognized and then come forward when acknowledged. The message in tongues could then be spoken through a microphone so that all could hear and all could profit. The same is true with interpretation of tongues.

If such people are being led by the Spirit of God, they will be able to hang on long enough to come to the front. If they can't do that, then something is wrong with their container, and they need to either work on it or start moving a little more quickly.

It is fine for a message given by God's servant to be explosive, but it needs to be controlled. As Scripture says, **The spirits of the prophets are subject to the prophets** (1 Corinthians 14:32). That means if the message is inspired by the Spirit of God, it can be controlled.

God's servants in the pulpit are flowing in a certain vein and they have the mind of God. There were times when people would come, raise their hand, then stand and wait to be recognized. If we did not give place to it, they would sit back down.

WHAT IF SOME FEELINGS GET HURT?
• • •

You might ask, "Has anybody ever gotten their feelings hurt when that person wasn't allowed to give a message during the church service?"

I remember one lady who was hurt by it, but she came to me later and apologized, saying she had a bad attitude. She said, "I couldn't understand why everything came from the platform." This was an opportunity for me to explain further about administration and operation of the gifts.

I said, "Let me ask you a question: did we ever allow you to vocalize that which the Spirit of God gave you?"

"Yes," she said, "several times."

"Then let me ask you this: when it comes to interpretation, have you ever noticed that there might be a heavier anointing on the one in the pulpit than there was on a message that you or someone else may have given?"

"Oh, yes," she said, "all of you have been doing it longer."

"Then if you are going to operate, you have an option. You can do it, or we can do it. We all know and hear the voice of God. Yet it comes down to determining who will do it. We made a determination that we wanted the message given to be as strong and powerful as possible, so we were led to give the interpretation."

She accepted and understood what I was saying.

The problem is, many times the pastor can get himself into trouble. Suppose somebody gives an utterance in tongues during a service and he waits thirty minutes for somebody else to give the interpretation. He will end up with a can of worms and will wish he had never had it, because when he lifts the lid, everything will come crawling out. Some people could be tempted to operate in the flesh and give something out from their mind and it not be God.

So, as the apostle Paul has said, there are differences of administrations and differences of operations in the gifts of the Spirit.

Now what is the principle in these examples?

That all may profit.

It is the Spirit of God Who is moving upon an individual when he or she does know the voice of God.

Now you can understand that different ministers or administrations operate on different levels of faith. But we have to know where and how we are to minister in these gifts, and then have some ethics about us so that we will do what is proper and right.

Let's continue now by discussing the third vocal gift: the gift of prophecy.

The Vocal Gifts:
The Gift of Prophecy
• • •

The gift of prophecy is the *greatest* of the vocal gifts. We find this gift mentioned over twenty times by the apostle Paul in 1 Corinthians, chapters 11-14.

EDIFICATION, EXHORTATION AND COMFORT
• • •

In chapter 14, verse 3, Paul says:

But he that prophesieth speaketh unto men to edification, and exhortation, and comfort.

Then in verse 4 he says:

...he that prophesieth edifieth the church.

We see, then, another of those *amazing sets of three*: the gift of prophecy is for *edification, exhortation* and *comfort*.

To edify means to build up or to charge up. To exhort means to give warnings or advice. To comfort means to cheer or to console. So a word of prophecy will build you up, will warn or advise you about something or will offer you comfort.

Whenever prophecy comes, it should do at least one of these three things: edify, exhort or comfort. Now I personally have found that for prophecy to really be accurate and on course, it will do all three: it will edify, it will exhort and it will comfort.

PROPHECY — THE HIGHER VALUE
・ ・ ・

As mentioned earlier, the gift of tongues is the least of these spiritual gifts. Then comes the gift of interpretation. Together, these two gifts are equal to prophecy, just as two nickels make a dime. The end result of those two should be the same as prophecy: for edification, exhortation and comfort. If a message in tongues and interpretation does not meet that qualification, it is not from the Spirit of God.

This means, then, that prophecy has been given a higher value than either tongues or interpretation. The gift of pro-phecy is entirely supernatural but is spoken in a natural tongue.

You should begin operating in these vocal gifts by speaking or singing in tongues, then going into the interpretation. After a period of time, when you feel more confident, you can begin to speak or sing out of your spirit by the spirit of prophecy.

When you first begin in this gift of prophecy, God will not lead you to immediately move into it at some great public gathering of people. This is a growing process. It is to be taken step by step, level by level.

But once the gift begins to develop and to grow and you find yourself in a public gathering, it will seem normal to you that the Spirit of God wants you to move forward with it. You will witness it in your heart. You will know it is the voice of God, and there will be a boldness and a confidence in your actions.

FROM THE SPIRIT, NOT THE MIND
• • •

Prophecy involves the human will and faith, but it does not involve the human intellect. The possessor of the gift controls the prophecy. **The spirits of the prophets are subject to the prophets** (1 Corinthians 14:32).

When a Christian is in church or in some gathering with other Christians and he speaks under a Holy Spirit anointing in the common language of those people, he is said to be prophesying. The speaker, whether man or woman, is anointed, directed and energized by the Holy Spirit.

An example of this is the exhortation Peter gave on the Day of Pentecost. *His words were without preparation.* His message flowed from his spirit rather than from his mind. Had he sought to prepare such a message, it would no doubt have been impossible.

Now remember this: a person cannot prophesy beyond his own knowledge. You will be able to go only as far as your knowledge of the Word. Therefore, faith is tied into it, and your knowledge of the Word becomes a key.

We must prophesy according to the proportion of our faith (Romans 12:6). For a person to prophesy events or occurrences which do not come to pass, he would be speaking beyond his faith.

Something else I want to point out about the gift of prophecy: it is not a ministry of criticism. It is not one person's opinion against another. It can, however, be a divine operation under the anointing of God to warn men and women of sin and of shortcomings so that they might alter their lives and be ready when Christ returns. This gift can lift a Christian out of his depressions, his negligence or his lukewarmness and bring him back into the mainstream of God's move.

Now there is the possibility that someone unlearned in spiritual gifts could be led by God to step out and speak a word of prophecy, which ministers life to those who hear, but that is the exception to the rule. It is most unusual for that to occur.

Let me give you an example.

WOMAN SPEAKS WORD OF PROPHECY FIRST BEFORE EVER SPEAKING IN TONGUES
• • •

One time in Oklahoma City, I was speaking at a Full Gospel Businessmen's Fellowship chapter meeting, and about thirteen people came forward to be filled with the Spirit. After I had given instructions and prayed a general prayer, I began to minister individually.

When I came to one lady, I said, "Now when I lay hands on you, the power of God is going to come on you, and you will be able to speak with other tongues." Then I put my hands on her and began to pray.

She didn't say anything, so I said, "Can you hear the words that are coming up inside you?"

She responded, "All I hear are words of English."

Now I recognized the Spirit of God, the voice of God, speaking up inside me and saying, *Tell her to go ahead and say that*. So I told her to say out loud what she was hearing inside.

She began to speak, but it was not in tongues; it was a word of prophecy. She began to say things that she didn't know about in the natural. Then once she had finished prophesying, she just started talking in tongues.

Now that might really blow your theology, but it was the Holy Spirit at work. As Paul had said to the Corinthian church, it was the same Spirit of God but a different operation (1 Corinthians 12:6).

You see, that lady didn't really believe in speaking in tongues, but the Spirit of God gave her that ability in a supernatural vein. When she began to prophesy, she told how her whole family would come to God and get born again — and they all did! Glory to God! What a way to start out!

MISUSE OF GIFTS IN A CHURCH
• • •

Unfortunately, there have been times when the gifts have been misused within the Body of Christ. Something that happened in one church that I know of, particularly comes to mind.

At the close of every message by the pastor, and before he could begin the altar call, one of the church members felt that it was her duty to give an utterance to the congregation. The word she gave always expressed the need of the people to get saved.

You might say, "What's wrong with that?"

For one thing, it was always taking away from that pastor's ministry. In effect, the woman was saying that her pastor and the Spirit of God together were not able to give an altar call that was good enough to get the people saved.

How unfortunate that the gifts of the Spirit can be taken and used in the wrong way.

PASTOR FEARFUL OF THE GIFTS
• • •

Now I became familiar with one minister who was not used very much in the gifts of the Spirit. As pastor, he filled the pulpit acceptably, but he was fearful when it came to interpreting a message in tongues or giving a word of prophecy.

Whenever someone in the congregation would begin to move in that way, he would get uptight. He felt that he could not control it because he wasn't used in that area, so he would go on the defensive about it.

He ran a really strict and tight reign on any gifts operating in his church. Needless to say, there was not much going on among those people with regard to the gifts of the Spirit.

My wife and I are used in these vocal gifts, and we felt led to minister at that man's church. But we have been taught that you don't cause a disturbance at a church. When the gifts are used, there is to be order. We would never want to get in the way and frustrate people just because we felt that we had something from God. So it became difficult for us to minister in that church because of its operation.

One thing about it though, if you have something from God, He will always give you a place to deliver it. If one person or group won't receive it, somebody else will; so you can sit on it. The problem is, you simply recognize that they have need of it, so you would like to obey God and go ahead and give it. And that would be understandable.

Now I don't feel that I failed God or missed Him, even though I sensed that the Spirit of God wanted to speak and to accomplish certain things. But God will not violate a person's conscience. And if God will not violate that person's conscience, what right do I have to violate it by stepping out of order and moving in the gifts of the Spirit?

You see, we have to understand authority. Unfortunately, there are lots of people who don't understand it. There are levels and types of authority. God is the Supreme Authority, the Word is the second authority, and man's conscience is the third authority. Any other authority under that is on a lower level.

So even if I am called and used of God, I don't have the right to come along and be used in the gifts if it violates another man's conscience. Now that may shock you, but if God won't violate it, how can I? You see, what that person needs is more knowledge of God's Word; his conscience needs to be changed.

What that pastor did was according to his own knowledge and experience. Even though he believed that the gifts of the Spirit were real, he did not have enough knowledge of the Word to cause him to feel comfortable and to go with the move of the Spirit of God through tongues and interpretation or prophecy. His obligation was to his congregation. He had authority in his church, and I had to recognize that fact. Because of his position, I could not supersede his authority.

The only authority that could override that pastor's authority would be if God Himself told me to go ahead and do it. But that is not likely. God would know how to deal with him.

Understand now, God will not place you in a position and give you higher authority without a reason, so He is not in the habit of bypassing another man's authority.

Now I don't want to leave a gray area in your thinking. You need to realize this: that pastor knows the voice of God and I know the voice of God, but he is at a different conscience level than I am. Because of his experience and his knowledge, he can only go so far in allowing certain things to move in his congregation, and I cannot violate that.

If God desired to reach one particular person in that church, He could move supernaturally for that one person without destroying everything there and hurting its pastor as a result.

****

In closing, let me point out that the vocal gifts allow you to know the voice of God. They open you up to hear, to comprehend, to understand the other gifts that will come.

Let's continue now by looking in detail at the next group: the revelation gifts.

CHAPTER 8

The Revelation Gifts
• • •

As pointed out previously, there are three revelation gifts: the word of wisdom, the word of knowledge and the discerning of spirits.

Now let me point out the fact that the gifts of the Spirit will work in conjunction with one another. They work in harmony together. It is the same Spirit of God, but in each situation there is the need for a different manifestation. Sometimes it is necessary to have a combination of gifts at work.

I am not breaking down this group of gifts by subject just to be technical. I do it so that you will be able to recognize when the Spirit of God is presenting something to you. You will realize that one of the gifts is in operation and will be able to understand when the Spirit of God is giving you something in the future and when a combination of the gifts is involved.

Now you will find that all of the teaching in the Bible is pointed or directed to the vocal gifts; there is very little instruction on the power gifts or the revelation gifts.

Why?

Because there is a mutual cooperation tied in between you and the Holy Spirit.

You see, you cannot give yourself the word of knowledge or the word of wisdom. If God doesn't give it to you, you won't get it. Now you might have some vain imaginations, but that would not be from God.

As to the vocal gifts, even though you are filled with the Spirit, there are some things that you can say out of your own spirit. So there is a vital need for instructions on the vocal gifts.

God gives the spiritual gifts to you as He wills. The vocal gifts have a lesser value than revelation gifts, and there will always be more things of lesser value.

These revelation gifts are of a higher grade than the power gifts (faith, miracles, healing). It usually takes the revelation gifts for us to point the power in the right direction so that it gets the job done. We can operate in these gifts, yet we cripple ourselves by thinking, *I can't do it.*

Let's stop and think about this for a moment.

God is going to operate differently through each one of us. He is not limited; we are the ones who limit the operation of spiritual gifts. We limit it with our thinking. We limit it with wrong ideas. We limit it with a lack of teaching. Thus, we can stop it from flowing through us.

God uses different people according to their level. If it is different from what you have ever seen before, you have to be cautious that you don't go negative. When this difference comes, if you are not careful, you will say, "That can't be God." Then you will miss it and stop the flow of God from working in your life.

There is an old saying, "God can speak a word, and we will make a sentence out of it." Have you ever done that? I know I have.

The Word of Wisdom
• • •

This gift of the word of wisdom always has to do with future knowledge.

Wisdom vs. Word of Wisdom

Now notice this gift is called the *word* of wisdom. The *word* of wisdom is not the same as the wisdom that is talked about in the epistle of James and other places in the Bible. It is the same Greek word used in the book of James and in 1 Corinthians, chapter 12, but the meaning that the Spirit of God is endeavoring to get across in each passage is different.

In 1 Corinthians 12, Paul is not talking about wisdom itself; he is talking about a word of God's wisdom.

As for wisdom itself, you have to understand that there are all kinds of wisdom. James 3:15 says there is a wisdom that is earthly and sensual and devilish; this is man's wisdom. But when talking about the word of wisdom in 1 Corinthians, chapter 12, we are talking about a portion or a fragment of God's wisdom.

Now there are two basic words for wisdom in the Greek: one is *sophia,* which has to do with insight into the true nature of things; the other is *phronesis,* which involves the area or the realm that will actually produce a specific result.[1]

A lot of people will come along and say, "Well, I just need some wisdom." They are saying that they need more common sense, more understanding. What man generally speaks of is wisdom, but the wisdom which the Word of God speaks about is totally different.

---

[1]*Vine,* p. 678.

You see, having the wisdom of God means having insight into the true nature of things. When God gives you a word of wisdom, He is not telling you what is happening now but what will happen in the future. The word of wisdom has nothing to do with what is happening right this minute; it always has to do with what will happen in the future.

This word of God's wisdom was often used in the Old Testament by both the major and the minor prophets. An example of this gift in the New Testament would be Acts 23:11, which says:

> **And the night following the Lord stood by him, and said, Be of good cheer, Paul: for as thou hast testified of me in Jerusalem, so must thou bear witness also at Rome.**

THE WORD OF KNOWLEDGE
• • •

This gift of the word of knowledge has to do with present or past knowledge.

Let me illustrate it by telling you how I first got started operating in the gifts of the Spirit.

As a young man when I first came into the things of God, I began by praying and meditating and studying the Bible. That was over thirty-five years ago. I hungered to know more about the gifts of the Spirit, so I read and studied every book that I could get my hands on. I yearned so much to see the spiritual gifts brought forth in my life. I can't tell you why this was so important to me. It was just something I craved, something I longed for. I wanted to see the gifts operate in my life, so I prayed and waited on God.

THE WORD OF KNOWLEDGE CAME FIRST

The first gifts I saw operating in my life to some degree were the vocal gifts. It was quite a while before I saw any other gift begin to work. Then one of the revelation gifts, the word of knowledge, started flowing; and each time that gift operated, it was in the realm of healing.

When this gift first began, a word would come to me in a meeting. The Spirit of God would speak to my heart that a person there had a particular condition, then I would name it.

Not being a doctor, I didn't know many medical conditions, and I certainly didn't know all of the medical terms. I would simply describe the condition that came to me as I felt led to do so by God's Spirit.

As I have found, much of the time God uses people according to their knowledge and their personality. That is why Scripture says there are differences of administrations and differences of operations (1 Corinthians 12:5,6).

It didn't do God much good to talk to me in medical terms because I didn't know what they meant. As a result, even if He spoke them to me, I wouldn't know what He was talking about because I wouldn't know the words. I would be fearful of speaking them out, afraid that I would mispronounce them. So for a time, such fear blocked me from moving in that vein.

But I would know when it came. The Spirit of the Lord would say to my heart, "There is a person here who has such-and-such condition." Then I would speak that out to those present.

I ministered the way God had told me to do it. Sometimes the Spirit of God would tell me to point to someone and say, "You are healed!" Other times I would lay hands on that person myself. Sometimes I would have people around them pray for them. People got healed by God, and I rejoiced!

After about a year, this gift of the word of knowledge began to operate a little differently through me. I would be preaching and all of a sudden I would feel symptoms in my body. I realized that was a way for me to know that somebody had that condition, so I would describe it to the people.

I think one of the reasons God gave me feelings that way is because I didn't know what to call it. So to get through to me and to bless the people in need, God would move on me in that fashion and I would describe the symptoms that I was feeling. When I called it out, those with that problem would raise their hand, be ministered to as God said and get healed.

So the gifts of the Spirit operated for me in just those two ways: the word of knowledge together with the gift of healing. I functioned that way for a number of years. Those gifts worked well, and I had great results. God really blessed me that way.

A NEW WAY

Then one day in November of 1977, God spoke to me supernaturally and dealt with me about starting Faith Christian Fellowship. He told me to go back to Tulsa (because I was in Michigan when He said this), start a family church and a charismatic teaching center and reach the world.

I said, "All right, Lord. But it's going to take a lot of people."

He said, "I will give you able workmen, cunning in all their craft."

"But, Lord, it's going to take more than what I've got in many other areas."

Then He said, "The word of knowledge is going to begin to operate in a new way."

I got excited about that. But as I said earlier, here is where God can speak a word and we can make a sentence out of it. And that's exactly what I did!

WAITING FOR GOD TO DO IT MY WAY

At one time I had seen a husband and wife in Florida who ministered so profoundly in the gifts of the Spirit. I will never forget the first time I ever saw them. It was amazing. This couple would come to the pulpit together, bow their heads and begin to pray.

The wife was particularly accurate and exact. She might say something like this: "There is a lady here who is red-headed, who is wearing a black skirt with a red-and-black blouse, and who has black beads and a gold chain around her neck." She would tell how tall the lady was and how much she weighed, then she would describe the physical condition the lady was having problems with.

When the wife had finished, nobody in the building was standing around scratching their heads, saying, "I wonder who that could be?" The description she had given was so accurate that everybody knew exactly who she was speaking of.

When the Spirit of the Lord had said to me that the word of knowledge would operate in "a new way" through me, I thought of that couple in Florida and said to myself, *That's me. Glory to God! I can't wait for this to happen!* I was really excited and looking forward to that.

So I waited. And I kept on waiting. In fact, I am still waiting. God has yet to operate that way through me.

There I was, so sure that the word of knowledge would operate in that way. Yet the Lord had said that when it operated, it would be in a new way. Then when it did begin to work, I almost missed it.

WORD OF KNOWLEDGE IN FINANCES

Our church, Faith Christian Fellowship, in Tulsa, Oklahoma, was about two months old. One Sunday morning, I was sitting on the platform during the offertory, praying in the Holy Ghost. All of a sudden, the Spirit of the Lord spoke to me and said, "One of My children just this week asked Me for a sewing machine. Say that."

I thought, *Dear God, that doesn't even sound spiritual. A sewing machine? What does that have to do with Sunday morning church?*

As that thought was running around in my mind, naturally this other thought came to me: *What if it isn't God? I'll look like a fool!* And I certainly didn't want that.

Then I had another thought: *But what if it is God and I don't do it? Then I **would** be a fool! So I asked myself, Would you rather **look** like a fool or **be** one?* I decided right then that I would run the risk of looking like one.

I stood up and said, "The Lord just spoke and told me that there is someone here who asked Him for a sewing machine."

A young lady on the third row raised her hand.

I thought, *Glory to God!*

Then all of a sudden, fear gripped my heart when the thought came, *What am I going to do now?*

But just as quickly, I heard the Spirit of the Lord speak inside me and say, "There is someone here who has a sewing machine to give away and didn't know what to do with it. Say that."

I knew I was hearing the voice of the Lord, so I spoke it out. I said, "The Lord told me that someone here has a sewing machine to give away and didn't know where to give it. Let me see your hand."

I looked around but didn't see a hand raised anywhere.

At that time we had an L-shaped auditorium that went to the back and then around on each side. We could only seat about 250-300 and were running 440. I was looking around all the walls. Then toward the back, where it was dark in the shadows, I saw a fellow leaning out with his hand raised.

I was thrilled! But I must admit, I wasn't really expecting a man to have a sewing machine. That seemed a little odd to me.

Then he grinned and said, "Pastor, it's all right. I'm a Singer sewing machine dealer. We had a promotion, there was one machine left over, and I didn't know where to give it until now."

You see, God works supernaturally!

That was the first time God began to deal with me about the word of knowledge in finances, and it almost blew me away. I had never seen anybody operate that way. I was used to God working through me in healing, but suddenly He was dealing in finances, a realm that was truly unique.

You see, that was the agreement I had with God when He first called me to pastor. He said, "I want you to say whatever I tell you to say, no matter how silly it may sound or how dumb you may feel."

Many times when I step into the pulpit, all I do is get up and repeat what I hear the Spirit of God say in my heart. You can understand that it takes a faith relationship between you and the Lord. But it also takes an awareness of working with the Holy Spirit so that you can move into that supernatural realm.

So when I began to call out things in this way, God would reveal to me that people did not have money to pay their utilities. I would call out the need, and someone would raise their hand. Then I would say to the congregation, "Go and minister to that person." People would go to them and hand them money to help pay the bills.

Hearing God's Voice

We have snow in Oklahoma, though not as severe as it can be in other parts of the country. But sometimes snow will turn to freezing rain and put a sheet of ice on the streets, which can become very treacherous.

I remember one church night when a freezing rain had hit our city and there weren't many people in the service. The Lord said to me, "Just this week, one of My children messed up the front end of his car. Speak that need to the group."

When I called out that situation, one guy raised his hand. He said that his car had slid on the roads and was broken down.

So I said, "Those of you who feel led, go and minister to him."

At the most, maybe six, seven or eight people responded. That bothered me. But I needed to get on into the Word, so I started preaching. I intended to talk with him after the service and ask if he had been given enough money to meet his need, but he got away before I could speak with him.

He came back the next Sunday, so I went to him and said, "Brother, when I called out your need the other night, I noticed that not many people went over to you. Did you get enough money to fix your car?"

"You know, Pastor, that was an interesting thing. The estimate to get it fixed was $143, and that's exactly what was handed to me."

You see, God can move so supernaturally when the people will hear His voice. It doesn't matter if one person had given that man $8 and another had given him $25. God was supernaturally meeting his need.

How did it come to pass?

By people knowing the Holy Ghost, having a personal relationship with Him, hearing His voice and then following His lead. That is spectacular.

Now those are the two areas where the word of knowledge came to me. Most people just operate with the word of knowledge in healing as I had done, so I was thrilled when it moved on into the area of finances as well. I have seen some wonderful blessings transpire over the years as I have operated in that vein.

A WORD OF KNOWLEDGE CAN LEAD TO MUCH MORE

I remember once when I was in Baltimore, Maryland, for a meeting. There had been a plane delay and all kinds of hassles; so by the time I got there, I was really tired and had to be in the service that night.

I knew that I needed to go to the hotel room to pray and rest and get quiet before the Lord. If I had not taken that time to rest but had reacted to all those outward elements, I would have been really uptight and not worth much once I was in the service.

When I got into my room, I fell back on the bed and started praying in tongues. Then all of a sudden I began to speak out words in English. These were the first words that came to me: "There will be a person tonight who has received some bad news."

When I heard this, I knew in my heart that God was speaking to me. It was amazing. But the words by themselves really made no sense to me.

I went to the service that night and preached a message from God's Word. Then when I came to the end and was getting ready to minister, the Spirit of the Lord spoke these words to me, "Say it now." So I said, "There's a man here who got some bad news."

A nice-looking black gentleman was sitting at the back, and I said, "Stand up, sir. The Lord told me to tell you that it won't be as bad as you thought. God is working on your behalf and He is going to change things right away."

As I looked at him, I knew something was going on within him. I said, "Come here, sir." When he walked to the front, I said, "You don't have the Holy Spirit, do you?"

"No," he said.

"Do you want it?"

"Yes."

I reached out, touched him and said, "Be filled with the Holy Ghost." He immediately raised his hands and started talking in tongues.

As it turned out, he was the pastor of a local denominational church. He would never have answered a call to come forward and get filled with the Holy Ghost had it not been for that word of knowledge which was directed specifically at him. God made a way for him to know that it was real. He was given a word of knowledge by a visiting minister who had no way of knowing about his personal life. So he knew then that it had to be from God!

"RAZOR BLADES!"

Another time when I was in Florida for a meeting, I was praying and seeking the Lord in the afternoon before the meeting began that night. As I was lying across the bed praying, the Holy Ghost suddenly said to me, "Razor blades! Razor blades! Say that tonight."

So that evening when it came time for personal ministry to the people, I said, "This should have meaning to someone: razor blades."

I looked around at all the people, but nobody responded. They were just sitting there looking back at me.

I said, "Well, I don't understand what this means. I don't know the interpretation, and I won't try to put any kind of meaning to it. The Spirit of the Lord just said, 'Razor blades.'"

Then a lady raised her hand.

I said, "Come here, honey," and she walked forward. Then I said, "What does that mean to you?"

"I use razor blades to cut corns out of my toes," she said.

Then God healed her foot!

Now stop and think about the uniqueness of God. He has so many ways to minister to people in so many areas. Let me give you another example.

"SWITCHES!"

I was to hold a meeting in a Spirit-filled church in St. Louis, Missouri. As I was lying on the bed that afternoon, praying in the Holy Ghost, the Lord said to me, "Switches!"

Now what did He mean by that? What kind of switches was He talking about? Did He mean railroad switches, or light switches, or switches that were used to spank children — or something else entirely?

When I got to the church service that night, I said, "The Lord spoke something to me today, and I'm supposed to say it to you. I know it has meaning to somebody. Here's what I heard: switches."

A young man in the back raised his hand.

"What does that mean to you, sir?" I said.

"Well, I'm an electrician and I put in thirty-five of those switches today."

I asked him to come forward, and as he was walking toward me, I could see that he was limping. I said, "Do you have a problem with your leg?"

"Yes," he said. "I fell off the ladder and hurt my back. It's hard for me to get up and down to do my work, and I was hurting really bad today. It would be hard for me to continue doing my job as long as I'm like this. I need help."

Then the Spirit of the Lord said for me to tell him what to do. I said, "The Spirit of the Lord says for you to stomp your foot on the ground. So do that." But when he did it, he just stepped down lightly with his foot.

I said, "No, do it hard." So he did it harder.

"Now do it again, and keep on doing it."

Pretty soon, he was jumping all across the platform and all around the auditorium. He got really excited, and the crowd was going wild. I found out later why everybody was so excited. It had to do with more than the fact that this young man got physically healed.

It seems that a few months before he had visited there from a denominational church, but he didn't like the way those people worshipped God. He had criticized the pastor for allowing them to do all that dancing and jumping and shouting and running. All that kind of behavior in church was just too wild for him.

This was the first time he had been back to one of their services. He had come because there was a special speaker. Then what does God do? He tells me by His Spirit to call out "switches." That was the first step to bringing healing to that man's injured body and then it led him to be filled with the Holy Ghost. As a result of that, he was bouncing all across the auditorium, rejoicing for what God had done for him.

THE DISCERNING OF SPIRITS
• • •

Let me define the gift of discerning of spirits. It means to be able to see into the realm of the spirit.

There has always been a big debate among people concerning this gift having to do with seeing and understanding the type of spirit that is involved.

There are no Bible instructions concerning how to use the discerning of spirits. Why? Because the discerning of spirits comes as the result of seeing in the spirit realm.

Either you see, or you don't see. Either you understand, or you don't understand. It is just that simple. But this gift is not to be used as the result of suspicion.

DISCERNING OF SPIRITS
WITH THE WORD OF KNOWLEDGE
• • •

Let me give you an illustration of the discerning of spirits. This is a personal instance, which has to do with the first time this gift ever operated in my ministry.

I was in a prayer meeting at a church in Muskogee, Oklahoma, which is where I had started my teaching ministry. A lady I had never seen before came to the service. She listened and was very attentive as I taught from God's Word.

When it came time to pray, I would take the different prayer requests and pray over them specifically. I used that as a way of teaching. I would demonstrate the kinds of prayer we could pray and show the kinds of results we could have. It was developing my ministry as well as teaching the people who had come to learn.

When I asked for specific prayer requests, that lady simply made this statement to me: "I want you to pray for my husband and me; we are having some marriage problems. I can't disclose just what." That was all she said.

I responded by saying, "Well, I believe the way we should pray about this is by praying in tongues. The reason we're going to pray in tongues is because there are so many unknown factors involved here. The only way I can deal with it is with the unknown."

You see, I didn't know enough about it to pray the prayer of faith or the prayer of commitment or the prayer of dedication. The only thing I knew to do was to pray in the Spirit.

I said, "Let's all join hands. We know that we will pray the perfect prayer according to the will of the Father." So we joined hands and began to pray in the Spirit.

As we were praying, all of a sudden I saw into the spirit realm. My eyes were closed, but my wife and some of the other people said the countenance of my face changed when I started to pray out loud while we were holding hands.

I could see that lady's husband and another woman. They were together at a motel in another city. He was standing to the left and she was to the right. She had a funny grin on her face and was holding her hands out toward him. Then I saw hundreds of strings or cords running out from her and wrapping all around him.

In the spirit realm I could see the man, the woman and the evil spirit that had them in bondage. I knew the name of the spirit that was at work in her, so the word of knowledge was in operation, too.

I didn't describe out loud what I was seeing in the spirit; I just called that spirit by name, took authority over it and broke its power in Jesus' name. The moment I spoke to that spirit, it was like an ax came down on all those strings or cords, and they just fell away.

When I spoke those words against that spirit, the wife threw up her hands right then and said, "He's free! He's free! He's free!"

You see, her spirit picked up on it immediately. That power was broken just as fast as you could snap your finger. We found out later that her husband came home that night, and their marriage was restored.

Now in that particular situation two gifts of the Spirit were in operation simultaneously: the discerning of spirits and the word of knowledge.

The discerning of spirits was in operation because I could see into the realm of the spirit. I could see their spirits, and I could even describe to you what that woman looked like.

The word of knowledge was in operation because I knew the name of the spirit that was operating in her. I knew the names of the town and of the motel where they were.

The word of knowledge is a portion of the knowledge of God about things present or past that were going on right then. The discerning of spirits is seeing into that realm of spirits and being able to deal and to perceive. So these gifts can be working together.

Some people think the discerning of spirits sees all evil, but that is not true. You might see evil spirits or human spirits or angels. You might even see the Spirit of God. You could know the kind of human spirit somebody has. That is why I say that the discerning of spirits is more than just seeing into the spirit realm. It is still seeing, but it goes over into perception.

Now let's look at the power gifts.

The Power Gifts

• • •

I want to spend a little time now on the power gifts, or action gifts. Again, the three power gifts are the gift of faith, the working of miracles and the gifts of healings. The most important of these is the gift of faith, because it takes more faith to receive a miracle than to work a miracle. Your senses are involved in working a miracle, but they are not when receiving. Let's look at it first.

THE GIFT OF FAITH

• • •

Now understand that when we speak of the gift of faith, we are talking about a supernatural manifestation of the power of God. The best way to define it would be to say that the gift of faith involves special faith to receive a miracle.

This is what makes a difference between faith and the working of miracles. The working of miracles achieves a miracle through another individual. With the gift of faith you can receive a miracle into your own life.

SAVING FAITH

Somebody asks, "What's the difference between this gift of faith and just regular faith, or saving faith?" The answer is simple.

Saving faith comes as a product of the Word of God. Romans 10:17 says, **So then faith cometh by hearing, and hearing by the word of God.** Saving faith comes by feeding upon the Word of God. The more Word you get, the higher level or degree of faith you will attain.

Let's look, for example, at what we call the fruit of the Spirit as mentioned in Galatians 5:22. One of these fruits is faith.

You say, "So what's the difference there?"

Faith is a fruit that grows in your spirit. It grows over a period of time by relationship and confidence and working with the Lord. Then it develops into a mature type of faith.

Saving faith is a product of the Word of God. The gift of faith, however, is beyond that; it receives a miracle by the Spirit of God. Let me give you an illustration that you might understand.

GIFT OF FAITH AT WORK

Do you remember the story of Daniel and the lions' den? After reading that story in the book of Daniel, chapter 6, everybody would most likely say, "Now, brother, that was a miracle!" Certainly it was a miracle, but it wasn't the working of miracles.

You see, there wasn't anything that Daniel did to get that miracle. There was no action on his part which would have caused it to come about.

What he did to hold shut that lion's mouth required faith that was beyond natural faith. No doubt he had faith in God. He had studied the Scripture. He knew God. He had a relationship with God. No doubt the fruit of faith was operative in his spirit. That faith was operative in him as a believer in Jehovah God.

But the faith that was at work at that moment was the gift of faith. It takes this gift of faith to receive a miracle from God when there is danger. In other words, there was no action involved from Daniel's standpoint to cause it to come about. He himself did not kill that lion. It took faith beyond his faith for him to do that.

You see, when you have believed God as far as you can, when you have gone as far as you can go, this is where the Holy Spirit takes hold and adds some faith to yours. It is a gift of God at that time. It is a manifestation of faith from God that is apart from your own faith.

So don't think for one moment that when it lists the gift of faith as one of the nine gifts of the Spirit it is talking about saving faith or about the fruit of faith. It is talking about receiving a miracle, primarily in a time of danger.

THE WORKING OF MIRACLES
• • •

The second power gift is the working of miracles. Now realize that faith is involved when it comes to working miracles. But it requires supernatural intervention in the course of ordinary events. God uses an earthly instrument to carry out His plan. So there is an action on the part of an individual to receive a miracle at that time.

JESUS FEEDING THE MULTITUDE

An example that you probably would be most familiar with was Jesus feeding the 5,000 (Mark 6:35-44).

Now you have to admit, that was a miracle. Yet it was the working of a miracle. It wasn't something Jesus received because He was in danger, like the gift of faith. Yet faith was involved in it; He had to have faith to do it. But it also took some action on His part. He had to take the bread and break it. He had to take the fish and divide it. He had to work the miracle in order to cause the multiplication of the food to come.

Let me give you another illustration.

SAMSON AND THE LION

What about in Judges 14:5,6 when Samson killed the lion? The Scripture says he didn't even tell his folks about it.

Now you might say, "But wasn't that the gift of faith? He received a miracle."

No. It would be the working of miracles. A miracle was wrought, but there was action involved.

You see, the gift of faith receives a miracle; but with the working of miracles, that miracle is worked through you. It is the power of God moving upon you at that time. You know, it had to be the power of God for Samson to kill a lion with his own bare hands. That was the working of miracles.

You can begin to see, then, that the gift of faith receives a miracle; the working of miracles works a miracle through an individual. But they both are involved in the miraculous.

THE GIFTS OF HEALINGS
• • •

The third power gift is the gifts of healings. Now over the years there has been a discussion of this gift because it is in the plural, *gifts of healings.*

When the gifts are listed in 1 Corinthians, chapter 12, verse 9, it says "gifts of healing." Yet further down in verse 28, it says "gifts of healings." It is plural in the Greek, so there are different gifts concerning healing.

HEALING SHOWS GOD'S MERCY

Now you will find that these gifts of healings are shown forth more in the New Testament than in the Old. Why is that? It is simple.

The Father-image of God and the mercy and grace of God were not revealed in the Old Testament. The Israelites did not have a Father-image of God. They had an image of an Almighty God Who would swat them if they got out of line.

It wasn't until Jesus came along and showed God's love that this Father-image was portrayed. Jesus said, **he that hath seen me hath seen the Father** (John 14:9). Then He went around healing and doing good. This was indicative of one thing: a showing forth of the mercy of God.

Now let me say this to you: these gifts of the Spirit will operate on behalf of the unbeliever as well as the believer. Did you ever think about that? Actually when it comes to gifts of healings, as F. F. Bosworth put it (his son quoted him when he was at my church), the Spirit of God will use them as a dinner bell to draw people in.

I have had this occur in my own ministry. Sinners have come into my services and have seen the word of knowledge

97

and the gifts of healings operate. After receiving healings themselves, they have come forward to be saved. That healing made them realize and know that God was real. So, like the phrase that Bosworth used, it was like a dinner bell, with God saying, "Come and get it!"

THIRTY-NINE GIFTS OF HEALINGS

As for the gifts of healings, I personally believe that there are thirty-nine different ones. The reason I believe this is because Jesus bore thirty-nine stripes. Also, I read that the American Medical Association has said that there are thirty-nine basic categories of sickness and disease. I have seen a number of them in operation, but I have never tried to count up all of it in my mind. I just know the various healings that God has done through me.

One time when I was in Norman, Oklahoma, the Spirit of the Lord said to me that somebody was there who had a growth or a knot on the back of the neck. I spoke that word of knowledge and said, "Who is that?"

In a moment, a boy about twelve years old raised his hand. He reached to the back of his neck and said, "I got one right back here, but it's not real big."

"Well, son, I don't care how big it is; God just said there's someone here who has that. I want to minister to you. Come on up here."

He came up and stood with his back to the congregation. I ran my finger around it to show the size of it and just exactly where it was. Because of the way he was standing, everybody could see it.

I was about to put my hand on it to pray and say, "Be healed," but before I could do that, it just disappeared! I didn't even get to pray!

Now when a fellow is all primed to pray the prayer of faith, it can be disappointing. But it let me know right away that I didn't have anything to do with it. God was in charge of it all!

DIFFERENT OPERATIONS

Now that gift of healing was a different operation than how it has been in other cases. So understand that there are going to be different operations in the different gifts, and it requires that we learn to cooperate with the Spirit of God.

There are different elements involved with healing. One has to do with your own faith. Another has to do with the faith of the individual being prayed for in some instances. Even though God is wanting to work miracles, even though He is wanting to bring healing, sometimes unbelief can get in the way. God can be willing to work a healing in people's lives, but sometimes there can be a hindrance. I will give you an example.

HINDRANCE CAN COME THROUGH ASSUMPTION

I was holding a three-day meeting in East Texas. On the second night when I came to the end of the service, I started to minister to some people. Then all of a sudden the Spirit of God began to move, and I had a vision in my spirit. I could see somebody wearing blue jeans and cowboy boots with one leg that was short, and I knew which leg it was.

I knew by the Spirit of God that I was to speak out what I had seen, so I said, "There's a fellow here who has on blue jeans and cowboy boots, and your right leg is short. God wants to minister to you, so come to the front."

Nobody moved.

I said, "Now I know I saw it. I know it's real. I know what the Spirit of God is dealing with me about. So come on."

Still, nobody came.

"For the last time," I said, "I know what I saw: blue jeans, cowboy boots and a right leg that's short. Fellow, get on down here."

But no one reacted to my call. There was nothing else I could do, so I just dropped it. Then we closed out the service.

The next night when I got ready to minister, again a quick flash came inside me of those blue jeans and cowboy boots. I said, "Last night the Lord gave me a word, but nobody responded. Now He has been merciful to give it to me again. This seems unusual to me, but God is giving somebody a second opportunity. Now, fellow, I know you're here. You have on blue jeans and cowboy boots and one leg is short, so come on down here."

Again, nobody moved.

By this time, my flesh was about to take control. I wanted to punch somebody out. I thought, *That fathead just won't come and receive from God!*

As that thought was going through my mind, a big gal stood up and said, "I ain't no feller, but I got a right leg that's short." When she stepped out from her seat, I saw that she had on blue jeans and cowboy boots just as I had seen in that vision.

Where did I make that mistake?

With an assumption.

Rather than saying exactly what I had seen in my vision, I had assumed that it was a man who was wearing those blue jeans and cowboy boots.

The Spirit of God wants to work miracles at times. You will have to learn how to work with Him. Take my advice and say exactly what He tells you to say. Don't add to it. Don't take away from it. Just say it like it is — no matter how dumb it may look or sound to you.

DIVERSITIES OF OPERATIONS IN HEALING
• • •

You know, in one ministry there will be an anointing for healing in a particular area, while another ministry will have an anointing for healing in another area. When you see that, you will realize how there can be differences of operations. Let me give you some examples.

✦✦✦✦✦✦✦✦

I knew one man who consistently had more people get healed of broken bones than anything else during his meetings. Somebody could come to him with a broken bone and be healed right away. Yet it was so seldom that anybody else got healed of other physical problems through his ministry.

Then I have seen Kenneth E. Hagin carry more anointing for healings in the area of such things as growths, hernias, tumors and goiters.

There was another minister that both Brother Hagin and I were aware of. He lived in East Texas, and he never went to any of the big churches. He held small, brush-arbor meetings. But he had an anointing for miracles that was really special.

God used him in this incredible way: he would spit in his hand and then rub that spit over the area of the body he was praying for.

One time Brother Hagin observed him ministering to a man who had a withered arm. He just spit in his hand and rubbed it all over that man's arm. Then that withered arm grew out and became the same length as the other!

****

Smith Wigglesworth was an individual who had a forceful type of personality. Many years ago, he was holding a meeting at the Assembly of God church in Dallas, Texas. As he was ministering, one woman who came forward was so big that she looked like she was eight or nine months pregnant. Her dress was protruding because of a large cancer growth in her stomach.

Wigglesworth was about to lay hands on her when the Spirit of God suddenly came upon him, and he began cursing that growth and punching her in the stomach with his fist. What he was really doing was hitting the devil in faith. Immediately, the woman grabbed herself and fell over a chair, doubled up in pain. She just lay there, crying, holding onto her stomach. Then Wigglesworth went on praying for other people.

After about fifteen minutes of ministering to others, he whirled around and pointed his finger toward that woman. When he did that, the growth in her stomach just disappeared!

Wigglesworth would often hit people and get them delivered. Needless to say, it would be pretty exciting to see that kind of thing happen; but are we supposed to use his method as our formula? I don't think so. That is a different operation. But it is the same Spirit of God.

****

When my wife, Pat, and I were in Phoenix, Arizona, I believe we had some of the greatest instant healings of any place we had ever been. At that time we were ministering to some prayer groups, and the people there were open for miracles. I love ministering to people like that. They are a delight and a blessing.

Pat and I had formed a prayer line, and we were going along together and ministering to the people. There was a tangible anointing. The gifts of the Spirit were operating, particularly through the word of knowledge and the gifts of healings. We would speak the word of faith over the people, and many of them were falling under the power of God.

All of a sudden I looked back and saw that Pat wasn't there. A lady had fallen under God's power and was lying on the floor. Pat had knelt down beside her. She was rubbing her hand up and down the woman's leg, from the ankle to about the middle of the thigh. Pat's eyes were closed, and she was praying in the Spirit. I could sense that an anointing was flowing, and I knew something special was happening.

I found out later that the lady had suffered from polio. One leg, which had not grown out properly, was smaller than the other.

I watched as Pat was praying for her. Suddenly, the short leg filled out to full size! Now that was a different kind of operation. But it certainly was exciting!

****

I was holding a meeting at a church in Shawnee, Oklahoma, where Roy Sprague was the pastor. During the preliminaries I was just sitting there on the platform when, all of a sudden, the Spirit of God began to move inside me.

Three different people in the congregation stood out before me. I knew the Spirit of God was wanting to show me something. He said in my spirit, "When you take the pulpit, I want you to minister to them before you preach."

When they had turned the service over to me, I said, "I have to obey the Lord. He just made me aware of three individuals, and I need to minister to them." Then I pointed out those three people and said, "Come, I want to minister to you."

The first lady marched down the aisle. I walked toward her and looked her in the face. All I could see at that moment was somebody lying in a casket. I didn't have any idea whether that meant spiritual death or physical death; and if it meant physical death, whether somebody had died or was going to die. I didn't know exactly how to handle it.

There I was. I knew the Spirit of God was moving at that moment and I was supposed to minister. I thought to myself, *Lord, what do I do?* All I had at that moment was a desire to pray in tongues. So I reached out, put my hand on her head and began to pray in the Spirit.

I went on praying in the Spirit for a few minutes when all of a sudden I just hit that place of victory. I began to laugh. Then she began to shout. We knew we had the answer. I said, "Well, hon, I don't understand it. But we've got the victory, don't we?"

"Yes, we do!" she said. Then she turned and marched back up the aisle, and I went on and ministered to the other two people as I felt led by the Spirit.

I left the service that night wondering what had gone on in the spirit realm. As I was riding home with Roy and his wife, Opal, I said, "You two won't believe what happened to me tonight."

Then Opal said so directly, "What did you see?"

"What makes you think I saw anything?" I said.

"You lost all of your color," she said.

Now stop and think for a moment. If you were looking in somebody's face and all of a sudden saw that some person was lying in a casket, you might lose your color, too. I mean, it just startled me. Now the Spirit of God may have tried to show me more or say more to me about the situation, but I was so shocked by what I had seen that, if He did, I just failed to pick up on it.

It is a matter of learning how to cooperate with the Spirit of God. That is what I want to get across to you. It can be genuine and valid, but we have to learn how to go with it.

I said, "When that woman stepped up in front of me, it was like I looked into a casket at a dead person's face."

Then Opal began to laugh. I said, "Now, Opal, it isn't funny."

"Buddy, I'm not laughing at you. You don't realize what was going on."

"No," I said, "I don't have any idea."

"You see, her daughter is on trial for murder, and she has to go on the witness stand tomorrow."

Then I thought to myself, *Now why couldn't the Lord just say that to me?*

You see, as the Scripture says, there is a diversity of operations. Now we entered into God's best that night because that woman got the victory. She was able then to go ahead and do what needed to be done.

****

Can you see the variety there can be in the spirit realm? The more you acquaint yourself with the Spirit of God and His ways, the more you will know that He is at work and you will bear witness to it; then you will be able to cooperate with Him when some situation presents itself to you.

Stay open to the supernatural realm. It is not natural; it is supernatural. It is not the norm. When God begins to utilize you in new ways, it might seem foreign to your mind, but it should register in your spirit because you know the voice of God.

CHAPTER 10

Operating the Gifts in Your Own Life
• • •

Let's read now from Ephesians, chapter 5:

> See then that ye walk circumspectly, not as fools, but as wise,
>
> Redeeming the time, because the days are evil.
>
> Wherefore be ye not unwise, but understanding what the will of the Lord is.
>
> And be not drunk with wine, wherein is excess; but be filled with the Spirit;
>
> Speaking to yourselves in psalms and hymns and spiritual songs, singing and making melody in your heart to the Lord;
>
> Giving thanks always for all things unto God and the Father in the name of our Lord Jesus Christ;
>
> Submitting yourselves one to another in the fear of God.
>
> **Ephesians 5:15-21**

Paul says in verse 15 that we are not to be fools but are to walk as wise men. Are you ready to do that? As he says in verse 16, we have to redeem the time because these days are evil.

Wherefore be ye not unwise, but understanding what the will of the Lord is (v. 17). God wants us to understand what the will of the Lord is. The Holy Ghost will teach us all truth and lead us into the will of God. We confess that Jesus is Lord by the Holy Ghost. Then He can take the Word of God and use it to get us into a place of understanding the will of God for our lives.

Sometimes it has been hard for me to determine the will of the Lord. There have been many occasions when I didn't know what the will of the Lord was. But God is long-suffering, patient and kind; He puts up with a lot. And I am so thankful for that.

But there are some things the Word says that are black and white. These things are really clear. Would you agree that we are obligated to walk according to God's Word? That is what God is saying here in this passage from Ephesians 5.

WHAT IS THE WILL OF THE LORD?
• • •

In Ephesians 5:17 God is telling us, "Don't be unwise, but understand what the will of the Lord is." So, what is the will of the Lord? He goes on to tell us in verse 18:

And be not drunk with wine, wherein is excess; but be filled with the Spirit.

God's will is for every believer to be filled with the Holy Spirit.

You might ask, "But why? What difference does it make?"

There are a lot of people who have received life by believing in Jesus, but they are not living the abundant life that He talks about in John 10:10, saying: **I am come that they might have life, and that they might have it more abundantly.**

God wants you to be filled with the Spirit. You have to decide whether you want to be carnal or spiritual. But you have to understand that abundance is more than just getting filled with the Spirit. For you to get to that abundance, to the place where it can really begin to affect your life, requires the Holy Ghost. You have to come into maturity. You have to develop in all the things that God wants you to have.

When it says here in Ephesians 5:18 that we are to be **filled with the Spirit,** a better way of saying it would be to say "be being filled" or "be continuously in the process of being filled with the Spirit." You see, it is one thing to get a glass full of water; it is another thing to keep that glass full.

God does not want you drunk on wine. What is God's will for you? To get drunk in the Holy Ghost. That is what He wants for every believer.

Is there a parallel in the Word of God for this? Yes. How about what happened to the believers in Acts, chapter 2, on the Day of Pentecost? Didn't the other people look at them that day and think they were all drunk? Peter had to explain it. He said, **For these are not drunken, as ye suppose** (v. 15). What had happened to them? They had been filled with the Holy Ghost.

BECOME "CAREFREE"
. . .

What is the characteristic of a drunkard? When he gets loaded, doesn't he become "carefree"?

What is the importance of getting drunk on the Holy Ghost? That is God's cure-all for your worries. The Bible says in 2 Peter 5:7 that you are to cast all of your care upon Him because He cares for you.

Many of us try to cast our care by saying, "Here's our care, Lord." But then two minutes later, we pick it back up again.

Why does a drunkard keep getting tanked up? So that he will be able to forget all of his problems and troubles. If he can just get drunk enough, he won't be able to remember them.

GET DRUNK IN THE SPIRIT
• • •

When you have gotten drunk, what is the difference between your spiritual man and your natural man?

Your natural man will have a hangover the next morning, and still have all those problems. But your spiritual man won't experience a hangover. Things will begin to change in your life when you have been praying the perfect prayer according to the will of the Father.

This is God's way of getting you free from all the burdens and cares and anxieties in your life. You open yourself to reach a place of victory by being filled with the Holy Spirit and speaking in other tongues. Then you are to keep on drinking of God's Spirit.

You see, the world is trying to drown itself with the bottle. But God wants you so full of the Spirit that you will be more conscious of Him than of anything else. It would be just you and the Lord.

I guess people are walking in the knowledge that they have. But they are treating the Holy Ghost like a smallpox shot, thinking that one shot does it all.

Some will say, "I got the Holy Ghost back in 1924, but I ain't done nothin' since." Why? Because they are not staying full of the Holy Ghost. Some of them are living on half a tank while others are staying close to empty. Then they wonder why their lives are dry and dull and dead. They wonder why they are not victorious but are living in despair. They are not living the abundant life because they don't stay full of the Holy Ghost. A drunkard can only remain drunk if he keeps on drinking and stays full.

You may get yourself a drink of water and be satisfied right then, but you will be thirsty again in a little while. If you intend to stay full, you have to keep on drinking.

The same is true if you want to stay full of the Holy Ghost: you have to keep on drinking in the Spirit. Believers should be constantly in the process of being filled.

STAY FILLED!
· · ·

As we have seen in Acts, chapter 2, the disciples were amongst the 120 who got filled with the Holy Spirit. Then later in Acts, chapter 4, it says that Peter was **filled with the Holy Ghost** (v. 8). So he was still filled.

But when the disciples went out and began to testify and witness and share with the people, they got into trouble and caught some flak. So they came together and had a prayer meeting. Notice Acts 4:31, which says:

> **And when they had prayed, the place was shaken where they were assembled together; and they were all filled with the Holy Ghost, and they spake the word of God with boldness.**

These were still the same disciples who got filled in Acts, chapter 2, and again in chapter 4. Then later in chapter 13, it says, **And the disciples were filled with joy, and with the Holy Ghost** (v. 52).

You might ask, "Well, exactly when did they get filled with the Spirit — in chapter 2, chapter 4 or chapter 13?"

In all three! They were constantly in the process of being filled!

So the way you stay full is to keep on drinking.

The problem is, when some believers get filled with the Holy Spirit they think they have arrived and they say, "Glory to God, I got it!" But then somewhere down the line life gets tougher and they feel miserable. Why? Because they have not allowed the Spirit of God to fully move in them.

For you to move in the supernatural realm and in the gifts of the Spirit effectively and efficiently, you will need to maintain the fullness of the Spirit of God. You need to pray in tongues on a regular basis, which means consistently, every day.

This is not a hit-and-miss process. If you want to really move in the supernatural realm, you have to do what is necessary to get there. I am not saying it can never operate through you. But for you to live in that realm on a continual basis, expecting the supernatural to happen in your life, requires that you maintain that level by spending time praying in tongues. That will allow the Holy Spirit to constantly fine-tune your spirit.

Acts 2:4 says that the believers were all filled with the Holy Ghost and began to speak with other tongues. So we stay full of God's Spirit when we keep on drinking from those spiritual waters.

You Have To Speak to Yourself
. . .

Again, Ephesians 5:18 says:

And be not drunk with wine, wherein is excess; but be filled with the Spirit.

How? Verse 19 tells us:

Speaking to yourselves in psalms and hymns and spiritual songs, singing and making melody in your heart to the Lord.

This verse doesn't say you are to speak to someone else. It says you are to speak to yourself.

Now don't get upset about talking to yourself. Did you know that someone in the Bible did that? It's true. The Bible says David did it. In 1 Samuel 30:6 it says David **encouraged himself in the Lord.**

If you are bothered about talking to yourself, I have news for you: if you don't say good words to yourself, there may be a time when you can't get anybody else to do it.

So it is important that you spend time with God in your own private devotions, in your own prayer life. I will demonstrate how you can allow this to work for you. You have to be willing to open the door wider and walk on into the gifts of the Spirit.

You must allow the Holy Spirit to work inside you. The more familiar you get with His presence and His prompting, and His moving upon your heart, the more comfortable you will feel. It is like driving a car. The more you do it, the more natural it feels to you. As the old saying goes, practice makes perfect. By entering in, there are certain exercises that you can do to avail yourself of these spiritual gifts.

It is the Holy Spirit Who will move inside you and cause this to happen. Yet as a believer, you have the capacity, or the potential, to allow these gifts to operate within you.

As I had mentioned earlier in this study, these spiritual gifts are like equipment that will help you carry out the work God wants you to do. You wouldn't send a man out to dig a ditch and not give him a shovel. So God is not going to make you responsible for something without giving you the necessary equipment. Whatever your job or position might be in the Body of Christ, God will equip you accordingly and help you to get that job done.

Remember we are working together with the Lord. But before He can work within us, we have to be doing something. That means we have to get involved through faith. Then the Holy Spirit will be able to move in and begin to manifest Himself.

So how does God operate through you?

First, you have to get filled with the Spirit and begin to speak in tongues.

What is the first spiritual gift you can operate in that will create life? Divers kinds of tongues. How do you maintain the fullness of the Spirit? By speaking to yourself in psalms and hymns and spiritual songs. Then God will begin to graduate you into other spiritual gifts as you maintain the fullness of the Spirit.

How This Happened to Me
• • •

Let me explain how this worked in my own life.

I began by speaking or singing in tongues during my private prayer time. Then after a while, I started interpreting what I was saying; and before long, I was willing and able to go on into prophecy.

How did I begin working this in my life? By speaking to myself. I spent this time encouraging myself. There were days when I felt so dull, so listless, so dry; but I had to go on and worship God in spite of the way I felt.

You might say, "Do you mean you actually talked to yourself?"

Yes, I did — and I still do!

Some people might get uptight and say, "But what if you start hearing answers?"

That's the whole idea!

You might be like lots of other people who need some answers. I want you to know that you don't have to be running all over the world looking for answers when the One Who knows it all is living right there inside you. That means you would be out there looking in all the wrong places. God has already given you everything you need by giving you the Holy Spirit; He is resident inside you.

I learned to look in God's Word. Then the Spirit of God, the One Who can unveil that Word, would lead me and guide me into the truth. As Scripture says, God's Spirit will teach us all things. Not *some* things. Not a *few* things. *All* things! He will work to bring us into that abundant life.

We can be carnal, or we can be spiritual. We can have life, or we can have the abundant life. I made the decision that I wanted the abundant life!

But for me to experience that abundance meant that I had to put something in; I had to make a deposit. You see, it is important that we spend time speaking encouraging words to ourselves. There may not be anybody else around to do it.

What had I accomplished by taking those steps privately? I had placed myself in a position to be used by God when He was ready to use me. Then out of my private time of being filled and staying full, I developed an overflow. I reached the place where I could be used publicly by God. If you are not willing to do this privately, you can't be used by God publicly. Forget it. It just won't work.

Have you ever felt that you needed this abundance in order to worship God? You should be worshipping the Lord every day. But did you ever get up in the morning and just not feel like it? You know you ought to be worshipping God, saying joyfully, "Glory to God! It's another day!" Instead, you only feel dryness, maybe even turmoil, frustration, desolation, despair. You can't give away something that you don't possess.

So what must you do first?

MAKE A SPIRITUAL DEPOSIT
• • •

You have to put something in. You have to make a deposit before you can withdraw. That's the way it is at your local bank, isn't it? Well, the same is true spiritually. Before you can draw out of that well, something has to be put inside it.

That is the job of the Holy Ghost, Who was given to you by God. He is the One Who helped you to confess Jesus as Lord, and He is the One Who will lead you into all truth. He is also the One Who will deposit Life, Light and Power inside you. Then you will be able to draw it out and worship God as you should.

You might say to God, "Well, I know I am supposed to worship You, but I just don't feel like it." Don't be talking to God like that.

Now there is no point in your thinking that you can con God. He knows what is going on down in your spirit. So you have to quit playing games. Don't get out there amongst the religious. Remember, you are to be spiritual, not religious. There is a distinct difference. God is not religious. Jesus was not religious. So God doesn't want you religious; He wants you spiritual.

What are you to do? You have to minister to Him.

How? First, you have to speak to yourself. You can do that by speaking in tongues and then interpreting it, or you can just prophesy. It depends on how fast you grow in the things of God.

Let's say the alarm goes off one morning and you feel like it is a blue Monday. You don't even want to get out of bed, much less worship God. You just want to pull the covers back up and say, "Give me five more minutes." What are you being confronted with? Dryness. Emptiness. Barrenness.

The only way you can get filled up is by making a deposit, and the Holy Ghost is there to help you do that. Remember, He was there in the beginning to help you confess Jesus as your Lord, so He will be there to help you make that deposit.

The way to enter into the gifts of the Spirit is to begin in your own private devotions by praying in tongues as I did. You can get so full of the Spirit that you will want to sing and make melody in your heart to the Lord. It will begin by your speaking or singing in other tongues. Then after a period of time, you will hear words of English coming up inside you. You will realize that that is the interpretation of the prayer language which you had been speaking or singing to yourself.

Now what is taking place? At that moment and at that time, by speaking or singing in the Spirit you are getting yourself all charged up and built up spiritually. Those things are happening in the spirit realm, but your mind is not getting that much out of it. Yet, when you begin to sing or speak the interpretation, your mind will become edified also.

THE INTERPRETATION MUST BE
IN LINE WITH GOD'S WORD
• • •

So you begin by speaking or singing in tongues; then the interpretation will come as you avail yourself of it and begin to speak those words. The Bible says we are to prove all things and hold fast that which is good (1 Thessalonians 5:21). As you begin to speak the interpretation, you have to judge it in line with the Word of God.

Now isn't it much better for you to learn by doing this in private before getting out into the public eye? You would be able to develop a confidence and know beyond a doubt when the Spirit of God is leading you to speak out in front of other people.

By doing this privately and building yourself up, you begin to hear those words and you allow them to come forth. Then when the Spirit of God moves upon you in a service, it will not seem strange to you; it will be a voice that you know, that you have confidence in, that you can trust. That is the way you begin.

When other people are using the gifts of the Spirit, are there times when you will know in your own spirit before it occurs that something is about to happen, that the Spirit of God is about to move? If so, that means your spirit bears witness with God's Spirit. There is a confidence and a knowing within you right then. You say to yourself, "Yes, that's it. That's the Spirit of God. I know that's right."

No matter who speaks those words, you are required to judge all the words that come forth; you don't judge the speaker's heart. You judge those words in line with God's Word. The Word of God is the final authority on the subject.

You see, you have the basis and foundation to open yourself up and then know whether that is the Spirit of God. Therefore, you can recognize the Spirit of God when it comes to the tongue and to its interpretation, or even moving on into prophecy.

The ability to speak such words will develop and grow as you allow it to operate through you. You are cultivating a working relationship with the Lord.

AN EXAMPLE
• • •

The Spirit of God has come to lead me into all truth, but I have to allow Him to do that. I begin by speaking or singing to myself — to my spirit, my soul, my body — and I say words such as this:

> It's time for you to get up today.
> It's time for you to get on the way.
>
> It's time for the Spirit of God to rise in you.
> He's going to see you all the way through.
>
> So you begin to sing a new song.
> You declare that nothing's wrong.
>
> Declare His power and His might.
> Then He'll bring you revelation and insight.
>
> So sing a song of victory;
> Take your time; take your liberty.

The power of God is going to work in you today.
You're going to have just what you say.

So, body, arise and you be strong.
You declare, "I'm going on."

So the power of God will work in your behalf.
You'll be rejoicing and you'll be full of laugh.

Stop and think what will happen when you begin speaking such words to yourself. I promise you, it will energize you. You will feel the anointing from your heart.

A WAY TO USE THE POWER OF GOD
• • •

Can you see that this is a way for you to bring forth the Holy Ghost? According to 1 John 2:27, the anointing abides within. He will bring it forth and make it effective in you, but you have to put it to use.

What is God trying to do with the gifts of the Spirit? He is trying to teach us and bring us to a place where we can use the power of the Holy Ghost. With that life in us, we can then minister unto Him and eventually to others.

Let's look again at Ephesians 5:19:

Speaking to yourselves in psalms and hymns and spiritual songs, singing and making melody in your heart to the Lord.

Who are you to speak to? Yourself. How? In psalms and hymns and spiritual songs, singing and making melody. Where? In your heart. To whom? God.

What must you do before you can minister to Him? You have to speak to yourself. You have to make a deposit. Then when you have something inside you, it will be easy for you to minister to Him from your heart. You can begin speaking words like this:

> I want to bless You, Lord, for another day.
> I want to bless You, Lord, as I walk my way.
>
> I want to bless You, Lord, and sing a brand-new song.
> I want to bless You, Lord, out amongst the throng.
>
> I'm going to sing the victory.
> I'm going to shout and take liberty.
>
> For the Spirit of the Lord, He's in me alway.
> Oh, bless You, Lord, I'm singing it all day.
>
> I want to bless You, Lord, with all my heart.
> I want to bless You, Lord, and tell You I'll never depart.
>
> I want to bless You, Lord, with a happy heart.
> I want to bless You, Lord, 'cause You give me a new start.

With help from the Holy Ghost, there can be a worship of God flowing out of you this way. God wants you to step up into that higher realm.

What happens when you speak to yourself? It puts you in a position to be able to minister to Him. What does that accomplish? When you speak to Him, He will speak back to you. It will be like a well springing up inside you. It will be a *rhema*[1] from heaven, bringing Life, Light and Power when it comes.

First, you speak or sing in tongues and then you interpret those tongues. The next step will be for you to move on

---

[1]Vine, p. 683.

into prophecy. All of a sudden God will put that desire inside you. It is like rivers of living waters. The well speaks of Life — sustaining Life. Those rivers speak of Power.

What does that bring? Colossians 3:16 says, **teaching and admonishing one another in psalms and hymns and spiritual songs, singing with grace in your hearts to the Lord.** That gives you something to give to the world.

GOD HAS AN ORDER
• • •

Let me show you there is an order. We have to understand it. If I take God's order, I speak to myself and minister to Him. Then He ministers back to me, and I can in turn minister to the Body of Christ. That sets the stage for taking God's anointing to the world and ministering to the sinner.

The order for us to follow in ministry is this: first to God; then to one another in the Body of Christ; then to the world. Each requires a different level of faith.

It takes less faith for us to speak and minister to God. It takes more faith to minister to one another. But it is easier to minister to another believer than to a sinner. It takes much more faith and much more power for us to reach out to the sinner. You must remember that God does everything decently and in order (1 Corinthians 14:40). If we break the order, then we break down the power of it.

Why is it important to understand this order? Because there are a lot of people trying to run the world when they can't even minister in the Church. Then you wonder why you get tripped up and become frustrated. If you can't minister in an atmosphere where someone loves you, you might as well forget about going out into the world. The people there despise you.

SHOWING GOD'S LIFE, LIGHT AND
POWER WHERE WE ARE
• • •

Think about it: What do you and I need, and what does the world need?

God's Life, Light and Power.

God has given us His gifts for that purpose.

But what have we done? We have refused to receive what God has given to us in the Body of Christ. We have said, "These spiritual gifts may work, but only through the pastor and maybe through one or two special people in the congregation."

But God wants these gifts to work in every one of us — including you!

God wants the gifts to work within our churches, but He also wants us to take them outside our church walls.

I remember one time when Pat and I were sitting in a restaurant with another couple and a young man. We had been to a Full Gospel Businessmen's Fellowship meeting and afterward had decided to stop for some refreshments.

The young lady said, "You wouldn't believe what happened to me tonight."

All of a sudden, the Holy Ghost told me what she was about to say, so I stopped her and said, "Don't say a word. Let me tell you." Then I started telling her what the Holy Ghost had said.

123

Her mouth fell open. She couldn't believe what she was hearing.

I didn't let her finish her dessert. I said, "Put that down. Let's go." So we left the table, I paid the bill and we walked outside to the car. The three of them sat in the backseat, while Pat and I were in the front. I was turned around with my arm laying over the headrest. Then I began telling them the other things that the Lord had said to me.

Suddenly, the woman made a lunge for my arm, and when she touched it, she got filled with the Holy Ghost and began talking in tongues. We had been sitting there in that restaurant and then went outside to the car, and the Holy Ghost moved through us right where we were!

What did He do? He brought Life, Light and Power to meet the need. And we didn't have to be inside a church for it to happen.

We can't be locking ourselves away from what God desires for the Church. We have to see the full impact and the full extent of what He intends. If we don't understand the tools and don't know how to operate them, we will never use them.

Wouldn't it be a shame for God to treat us the way we treat some people? Suppose we were to hire a ditchdigger, give him a spoon and say, "Go dig that ditch six feet wide and ten feet deep." He could be working at it for a lifetime and never get the job done.

God is not unjust. When He calls you to do a job, He will give you the equipment to do it. But you have to be willing to open yourself up to Him.

Most of the time we haven't known how to do it because we haven't understood order. As a result we have never moved in it and haven't even known what it was for. But I am telling you now, it is Life, Light and Power that God wants to work in you and through you. And He wants the whole world to be affected by it.

We have to come together to minister and bless one another. First, we minister to Him. Then we minister to one another. Then we are to go out into this lost and dying world. Until we have a vision of that outreach to the world, we won't have the full heart of God. He died for those people out there. And what do they need? Life, Light and Power.

ALL THAT YOU NEED IS IN YOU NOW!
• • •

I have news for you: you are the one who has what it takes to get the job done. You can't be waiting on something else. Everything you need is inside you right now.

As you walk in the power of the Holy Ghost, He will lead you into all truth. You have to avail yourself of the Word in order for the Spirit of God to teach you, to direct you, to guide you. But when you do, He will make it real to you and cause you to understand. Then you will be able to go to the heights that God wants you to reach.

Remember, you can't prophesy beyond your own knowledge of the Word. So you have to begin by taking your knowledge of the Word and making melody in your heart to the Lord. As you cultivate and develop it, you will produce a flow and be able to go further. Then when you are in a believers' meeting or a church service and feel that you have an utterance, it will be much easier for you to act on it.

But let me give you some advice: if you haven't operated this gift in private, don't attempt it in public.

God will work through every individual who will avail himself of the Spirit of God. So, be filled with the Spirit. If you will spend time praying in tongues and singing in tongues, the Spirit of God will fill you up inside.

Remember, Romans 5:5 says that **the love of God is shed abroad in our hearts by the Holy Ghost.** When you pray in tongues, God's love will just well up on the inside of you.

Now God's love is already there because God is love (1 John 4:16). He came to abide in you when you accepted Jesus as the Lord and Savior of your life. But when you pray in tongues, you allow that love to be shed abroad. You enlarge it. When you become so conscious of it, there won't be any room for fear. **Perfect love casteth out fear** (1 John 4:18).

God's love will begin to work inside you. Then when that fear is dispelled from you, and His love rises up inside you, it will be easy for you to sing love songs to Jesus. Once you have spoken in tongues and begin to give the interpretation of tongues, you can then move on into prophecy.

As you allow the Spirit of God to stir up inside you in your private devotions, singing and making melody in your heart to the Lord, it can just begin to flow. You might start singing words like this:

The Lord is leading; He's guiding my soul.
He's healed my body; He's made me whole.
I sing a new song; I sing of His grace.
Oh, glory be to Jesus, one day I'll see His face.

You start telling God how great He is, how mighty He is, and He will show Himself mighty in your life. He will move by His Holy Spirit through you to begin to work as He wills to do.

As we have read in 1 Corinthians, chapter 12, verses 7 and 11, these gifts are to operate in *every* man. Don't be palming them off onto somebody else. You have to operate in what God intends for you to do. That is scriptural.

Scripture says in 2 Corinthians 10:4, **The weapons of our warfare are not carnal, but mighty through God to the pulling down of strong holds.** God can pull down these strongholds in our minds, our bodies and our spirits. He can destroy all the works of the devil and of the flesh.

As has been pointed out in this study, life started with the Father. He gave His life to the Son. Then the Son came to earth and gave His life that we might have that life. John 10:10 tells us how Jesus came that we might have life and have it more abundantly. The Holy Spirit was sent to bring forth that abundant life in us by bringing us into the Light and the Power by baptizing us with the Holy Ghost and power (Acts 1:8).

When you receive all that has been done, then that Life, Light and Power is made resident in you. When He gets you that full of the abundant life, then you can go and pour it out onto other people.

You have to start realizing the power that is involved in your life when you open yourself to the supernatural. What are you to present to the world? Life, Light and Power.

Through the vocal gifts you show people the Life of God — the Word of Life for them to hear.

Through the revelation gifts you show them the Light of God — the Light of Life for them to see.

Through the power gifts you show them the Power of God that will change their lives.

Through these gifts you might be helping to get people filled with the Spirit; you might be helping to get them healed; you might be helping to bring forth a miracle in their lives. God can cause all these things to come to pass through you. They can begin to operate effectively, freely and powerfully through you as you are willing to obey the move of God's Spirit.

About the Author

Ask **Buddy Harrison** who he is, and he will tell you, "I am a child of God, a son of God and an heir of God." Ask him what he does, and he will say, "I preach the Gospel — by sermon, book and tape." If he never preached another word, he knows he would still affect the world through prayer and the printed page. Because Buddy Harrison knows who he is in Christ and God's purpose for his life, he walks with assurance, ministers with a confidence and preaches with boldness and apostolic authority.

Numerous times in his life, Buddy has witnessed the miraculous, supernatural power of God. (As a small boy, he was healed of polio.) He has watched God heal, restore and deliver in his life and in the lives of those he has ministered to. He and his wife, Pat, move in the gifts of the Spirit with a sensitivity and an understanding.

More than thirty years ago, Buddy answered the call of God on his life and began his ministry in the ministry of helps as a music leader and youth minister. Today through the ministry of Faith Christian Fellowship International and the publishing company of Harrison House, Buddy is still in the ministry of helps. Both the ministry and the publishing company help men and women fulfill the call of God on their lives.

Buddy and Pat are known around the world for their anointed teachings from the Word of God and for their ability to communicate principles from the Word with a New Testament love. Because he purposes to obey God's Word and Spirit, Buddy has enjoyed tremendous success and favor.

To contact Buddy Harrison, write:

Buddy Harrison
P. O. Box 35443
Tulsa, OK 74153

*Please include your prayer requests
and comments when you write.*

Other Books by Buddy Harrison

Seven Steps to a Quality Decision

Man, Husband, Father

Four Keys to Power

How To Raise Your Kids in Troubled Times

Petitioning for the Impossible
The Prayer of Supplication

Understanding Authority for Effective Leadership

Getting in Position to Receive

Maintaining a Spirit-Filled Life

Just Do It

Count It All Joy
Eight Keys to Victory in
Times of Temptations, Tests and Trials
Coauthored by Van Gale

The Force of Mercy
The Gift Before and Beyond Faith
Coauthored by Michael Landsman

Available from your local bookstore.

HARRISON HOUSE
Tulsa, Oklahoma 74153

For copies of this book
in Canada contact:

Word Alive
P. O. Box 670
Niverville, Manitoba
CANADA R0A 1E0

The Harrison House Vision

Proclaiming the truth and the power
Of the Gospel of Jesus Christ
With excellence;

Challenging Christians to
Live victoriously,
Grow spiritually,
Know God intimately.